HOW TO BE HAPPY

HOW TO BE HAPPY

by David Lewis

JOSEF WEINBERGER PLAYS

LONDON

HOW TO BE HAPPY
First published in 2011
by Josef Weinberger Ltd
12-14 Mortimer Street, London W1T 3JJ
www.josef-weinberger.com / plays@jwmail.co.uk

Copyright © 2011 by David Lewis

The author asserts his moral right to be identified as the author of the work.

ISBN: 978 0 85676 341 0

This play is protected by Copyright. According to Copyright Law, no public performance or reading of a protected play or part of that play may be given without prior authorization from Josef Weinberger Plays, as agent for the Copyright Owners.

From time to time it is necessary to restrict or even withdraw the rights of certain plays. **It is therefore essential to check with us before making a commitment to produce a play. NO PERFORMANCE MAY BE GIVEN WITHOUT A LICENCE**

AMATEUR PRODUCTIONS

Royalties are due at least one calendar month prior to the first performance. A royalty quotation will be issued upon receipt of the following details:

Name of Licensee
Play Title
Place of Performance
Dates and Number of Performances
Audience Capacity and ticket price(s)

PROFESSIONAL PRODUCTIONS

All enquiries regarding professional rights should be addressed to Josef Weinberger Ltd at the address above. All other rights should be addressed to the author, c/o Josef Weinberger Ltd.

OVERSEAS PRODUCTIONS

Applications for productions overseas should be made to our local authorised agents. Further information can be found on our website or in our printed Catalogue of Plays.

CONDITIONS OF SALE

This book is sold subject to the condition that it shall not by way of trade or otherwise be re-sold, hired out, circulated or distributed without prior consent of the Publisher. **Reproduction of the text either in whole or part and by any means is strictly forbidden.**

Printed by Good News Digital Books, Stevenage

How to be Happy was first presented by the Orange Tree Theatre, Richmond (Sam Walters, Artistic Director) on 5th October 2011. The cast was as follows:

PAUL	Paul Kemp
EMMA	Kate Miles
GRAHAM	Steven Elder
KATY	Carolyn Backhouse
DAISY	Kate Lamb

Directed by David Lewis
Designed by Sam Dowson
Lighting Design by John Harris
Deputy Stage Manager – Becky Flisher
Assistant Directors – Polina Kalinina, Karima Setohy

CHARACTERS

Paul	Mid-forties
Emma	Early forties
Graham	Early forties
Katy	Mid-forties
Daisy	Eighteen, almost

ACT ONE

Scene One

The set is a contemporary living space, neutral tones, white wooden floorboards, some tasteful soft furnishings. An impressive sofa dominates the room which, somehow, does not look like a room. It is, in fact, a combination of two similar living rooms: one in EMMA *and* GRAHAM'S *home and the other in* PAUL *and* KATY'S. *It is not possible to tell where one room ends and another begins or which item belongs in which home.*

Necessary items include a couple of chairs, a non-descript coffee table and a baby monitor. Five or six remote controls lie on coffee table. They are used occasionally but hi-fi and television are beyond the 'fourth wall', therefore not visible.

It is night, the early hours of the morning.

> PAUL *is slumped on the sofa, alone, in semi-darkness. He is playing a game on his iPhone; comical sound effects can be heard. A glass on the coffee table contains a small amount of neat whiskey. Next to the glass are some papers pertaining to insurance, mortgage etc.*

Soon, EMMA *enters and sits right next to* PAUL *on the sofa, but they are unaware of each other.* EMMA *is wearing a dressing gown. She seems very tired, but uptight, on edge.*

For a short time, PAUL *and* EMMA *sit together (though they are in different homes).* PAUL *is involved in his game;* EMMA *is distracted, troubled.*

Crying is heard over the baby monitor. PAUL *does not react but* EMMA *sighs deeply. She hesitates, eyes closed, then leaves the room.*

> KATY *enters wearing a kimono-style dressing-gown. She has brushed her*

	hair. (She tries to look her best, even in the dead of night.)
KATY	Sweetie?
	(PAUL *doesn't respond, continues playing. She sits next to him, where* EMMA *was sitting. She checks her watch.*)
PAUL	(*mumbles, almost inaudibly, as he plays*) Nearly got . . . three stars . . . On all levels . . .
KATY	It's two-thirty.
	(*Pause. Then* PAUL *stops playing.*)

(*But we can still hear the baby crying.*)

	(*He looks at her. She returns his gaze. Some unspoken communication.*)
PAUL	(*matter-of-fact*) I'm fine. Honestly. I'm fine.
	(*She strokes his head tenderly.*)

(*The crying stops.*)

KATY	(*re: the papers*) What's all that?
PAUL	Yeah, I checked the insurance policy and it's all fine. (KATY *sighs, looks away, doesn't want to talk about it.*) It'll clear the debts. Plus about half the mortgage, so . . . (*Pause. Further looks exchanged.*) It's important.
KATY	Yes, I know, but . . . (*Pause.*) It's not really.
PAUL	You go to bed.
KATY	It's really not that important.

PAUL	I'm fine. Honestly. (*Pause.*) You go to bed. I'll be up in a minute.

>	(KATY *kisses him and leaves the room. Pause.* PAUL *sips some whiskey then stares into space. He picks up a remote control and presses a couple of buttons. Softly, 'Gute Nacht' from Schubert's 'Winterreise' is heard, the Hans Hotter and Michael Raucheisen recording.*)

(EMMA *enters and begins shuffling aimlessly around the room. She is fraught, drained, desperate.* PAUL *is unaware of her presence. Finally she sits next to* PAUL *and lowers her head into her hands.* GRAHAM, *wearing pyjamas, enters.*)

GRAHAM	What are you doing?

EMMA	Nothing. Let's go to bed.

(*She exits swiftly. He switches off the baby monitor then follows.*)

>	(*The music continues.* PAUL *is sinking into the sofa and into depression. He decides to return to his game. Lights fade to black.*)

Scene Two

A moment later, it is the next day.

>	DAISY *enters, followed by* PAUL. DAISY *is a striking young woman, stylishly, fashionably dressed although there is a good deal of black and a hint of the Gothic in her outfit.*

DAISY	I can't stand it anymore.

(*She takes off her coat and discards it.*)

DAISY	Jack doesn't sleep and cries, like, all the time! (*We hear a baby crying offstage.*) Why have another baby at her age? It's totally stupid! And they're constantly arguing!

(PAUL *stares.*)

(EMMA *enters and walks swiftly across the stage.*)

EMMA	(*stressed, irritated*) Graham, I thought you were going shopping.
DAISY	Dad, I'm serious;
GRAHAM	(*off*) I did.
DAISY	I can't stand it.
GRAHAM	(*off*) I've been.
DAISY	If Graham's not moving out, I'm moving out!
EMMA	Well, where's the milk? We need milk? (*She exits.*)
PAUL	Why would Graham move out?
GRAHAM	(*off*) I got milk!
DAISY	He's bound to eventually! That's, like, obvious! They hate each other!
EMMA	(*off*) Well, where is it?
PAUL	Daisy, darling, it's not that simple. There are children involved.
DAISY	One child! I'm not a child!
PAUL	No. Okay.

DAISY	And that's no reason to stay together.
PAUL	I have a great book, actually. (*He exits. Off:*) How to get your child to sleep. You could give it to your mother.

(EMMA *returns with two reusable canvas carrier bags full of groceries.*)

DAISY	I don't want to get involved. (*She slumps onto the sofa.*)
EMMA	Please can you put things in the fridge?!
DAISY	They're worse than me and Wayne.
EMMA	And not just leave them by the door! (*She begins searching through the bags.*)
PAUL	(*off*) How is Wayne?
DAISY	He's an arsehole.
EMMA	(*under her breath*) Wrong butter . . .
DAISY	Like you and Mum told me.
EMMA	. . . as per fucking usual . . .
PAUL	(*off*) Nobody thinks he's an arsehole.
DAISY	We've got a sofa like this.

(EMMA *places one bag onto the sofa, next to* DAISY, *and searches more thoroughly.*)

(PAUL *enters with the book.*)

PAUL	Really?
DAISY	Yeah, like, exactly. Exactly the same.
PAUL	Since when?
DAISY	(*shrug*) Don't know. Not long.

(EMMA *discovers an ostentatious jar of face cream and studies it, frowning.*)

(PAUL *offers the book but* DAISY, *surveying the room, ignores it.*)

DAISY   She's good at all this, isn't she? Katy.

PAUL   All what?

DAISY   Interior décor or whatever. I think Mum copies her.

PAUL   Really?

(EMMA *takes the rest of the groceries out to the kitchen.*)

DAISY   Yeah, I reckon she's jealous. (*Monitors* PAUL's *reaction.*)

PAUL   Of what?

DAISY   It always looks like a magazine in here.

PAUL   Yeah, well, she's a victim of consumer culture but she knows she is. She's well aware of that tendency, you know, to buy stuff she doesn't need, with money she doesn't have, to impress people she doesn't like.

DAISY   (*stares*) Doesn't like who? She doesn't like Mum?

PAUL   No, no, it's just a saying. It's a . . . universal truth.

DAISY   When's your new novel coming out? *Red Penguin*.

PAUL   *Blue Penguin*. I don't know. There's no actual . . . date yet.

DAISY   My friends are all buying copies.

PAUL	Really? Great.
DAISY	You'd think she'd have, like, learned her lesson!
PAUL	Who?
DAISY	Mum. She hates being a mother.
PAUL	(*thrown*) No, that's not true.
DAISY	Dad, she hates it! So, would I. I'm never having kids. It's a total nightmare.
PAUL	Darling, that's not true. She loved being a mother. She really did.
DAISY	D'you want to see my new car? (*She moves towards the door.*)
PAUL	(*beat*) You got it already?
DAISY	My birthday's next week. (*They exchange a look.*) All right, I'm a spoilt brat, I know I am.
PAUL	No, you're not.
	(*He puts the 'Get Your Baby to Sleep' book on the coffee table and collects up the papers from the night before.*)
PAUL	I ordered those balloons, by the way.
DAISY	Oh, excellent! I was telling my psychology teacher. What's the guy's name again?
PAUL	Albert Ellis.
DAISY	Ellis! Oh, yeah, I couldn't remember.
PAUL	American. Cognitive psychologist.

DAISY	He thought people expected the world to satisfy their ... desires or whatever.
PAUL	That's right. And you can't control the world. You can only control how you react to it.
DAISY	It's like the culture of entitlement.
PAUL	Exactly. He suggested these huge balloons floating over every town with three basic reminders on them.
DAISY	'Failure is more common than success'. (*Re: one of the letters he is holding.*) You got money with HSBC?
PAUL	Um ... No. Mortgage.
DAISY	Graham's got investment accounts. Six. Hundred. Thousand. Pounds. Sterling. (*Pause.* PAUL *stares, motionless, expressionless.*) I shit you not. Over six hundred thousand. HSBC. Three different accounts. (*Pause.* PAUL *is still staring, frozen.*) Sorry. Should I not have told you?
PAUL	(*shrugs it off*) No, no. Why? No, that's fine. None of my business. How d'you know?
DAISY	(*beat, shrug*) I make it my business to know. 'Failure is more common than success'. What are the other ones? (PAUL *is staring into space.*) Something about people liking you ...
PAUL	Um ... (*Pause.*)
DAISY	Albert Ellis. The balloons.
PAUL	Yeah. 'Whatever you do, many will dislike you'.

DAISY		Excellent.
PAUL		And 'The world does not oblige'.
DAISY		'The world does not oblige'. I love it! How many are you getting?
PAUL		Fifty. Standard. Plus a few helium.
DAISY		I can't wait to see my friends' faces.
GRAHAM	(*off*) Emma?	
PAUL		Do you think Graham will mind?
DAISY		(*beat*) What d'you mean?
PAUL		He's paying for the whole thing, isn't he?
DAISY		It's my party. I can do what I like. Come see my car. Actually, I got a present for you too. (*She smiles.*)
GRAHAM	(*off*) Em?	
PAUL		Really?
EMMA	(*off*) What?	
DAISY		It's pretty cool. Come see.
GRAHAM	(*off*) Come and see this.	
PAUL		Where is it?

(EMMA *enters and sits on the sofa.*)

DAISY		In the car. It's kind of . . . enormous.
EMMA	I'd rather not.	

(PAUL *is intrigued. He and* DAISY *exit. He takes the paperwork with him.*)

GRAHAM	(*off*) I'm looking at my brain. It's extraordinary.	

EMMA	I can't look at you. There's something . . . disturbing. You don't look human.
	(GRAHAM *enters, carrying a laptop computer and wearing an EEG (electroencephalography) cap. This resembles a swimming cap with numerous wires sticking out of it. It is connected, circuitously, to the laptop which displays an image of* GRAHAM'S *brain. Certain parts of* GRAHAM'S *brain are illuminated.*)
GRAHAM	Look at this. (*He places the laptop on the coffee table.*) That's the . . . Frontal Lobe.
EMMA	(*slightly disturbed*) Right.
GRAHAM	When we did this with Tammy, it looked like her Pre-frontal Cortex was throbbing.
EMMA	(*looks at him*) Tammy?
GRAHAM	Which has a lot to do with personality.
EMMA	She showed you her brain?
GRAHAM	Fascinating, isn't it?
EMMA	Does she show all the boys?
GRAHAM	I'll have to take a crash course in neurology.
EMMA	Why?
GRAHAM	This is the next big thing – or, rather, the new big thing – in advertising. We don't know enough about how and why consumers make spending decisions. What to buy. And what not to buy.
EMMA	(*a thought occurs*) Oh! Since you mention it . . . (*Exits to the kitchen.*)
GRAHAM	If you do a taste test with Pepsi and Coca-Cola, but you don't tell people which is which, most prefer Pepsi. But if they know what they're drinking, most prefer Coke. Ask them why, they'll

	say 'because it tastes better'. But it doesn't. It's a real deep-seated brand loyalty.
	(EMMA *returns, with the face cream.*)
EMMA	Why did you buy this?
GRAHAM	(*not listening*) People don't know their own minds. So, there's no point asking them. You have to get into their brains. See if you can find the holy grail: the consumer's buy button.
EMMA	Did you find Tammy's buy button?
	(GRAHAM *declines to answer.*)
EMMA	It's extremely expensive face cream. One hundred and twenty pounds for . . . (*Squints at the label.*) . . . 'Advanced Poly-collagen Peptide' something or other.
GRAHAM	I like buying you things.
EMMA	Well, I appreciate that. But I just asked for a cheap moisturiser. Where did you get this? They don't sell this in Waitrose.
GRAHAM	I don't know. Debenhams, I think. Next door.
EMMA	It isn't next door. It's across the street. A dual carriageway. Why did you do that?
GRAHAM	(*rather thrown*) Sorry?
EMMA	Why did you bother crossing the road?
GRAHAM	(*beat*) To get to the other side. This sounds like a chicken joke.
EMMA	Why go out of your way? And spend so much money? (*He stares. Beat.*) It's very nice of you, but . . .
GRAHAM	I'll take it back if you like. I suppose it's brand loyalty.

EMMA   To this?!

GRAHAM   Samantha swore by it. They did brain scans on a group of Carmelite nuns a while back.

EMMA   (*frown*) Nuns?

GRAHAM   Asked them to think about profound religious experiences. Turns out it's the same kind of brain activity whether people are thinking about God or about Ferrari or iPod or Guinness . . .

EMMA   (*under-whelmed*) Well, maybe, brain scans are too superficial. I mean, is that thing really going to be of any actual use to you?

GRAHAM   It might be. Yeah, maybe in the chocolate campaign. They studied the relative effects of chocolate and kissing. You know, what chocolate does to the brain versus what kissing does.

EMMA   With nuns?!

GRAHAM   No, different study. Turns out chocolate gives you more of a brain buzz than kissing.

EMMA   Depends who you're kissing.

GRAHAM   Sure.

EMMA   I mean, if you're kissing a nun.

GRAHAM   Actually, the nun study, I think they used MRI scanners. You get a better brain image but they're huge machines and you have to be immobile.

EMMA   I thought that was an MRI thing.

GRAHAM   No, it's an electro cap. Electroencephalography. EEG for short. They're great. You can send people shopping with these things on.

EMMA   Why would you do that?

GRAHAM   To see what shopping does to the brain.

EMMA	Or what public humiliation does to the brain.
GRAHAM	No, you can get electro caps which don't look like this. They don't have wires sticking out.

(DAISY *and* PAUL *enter. They are carrying – with some difficulty – a life-size, free-standing, cardboard cut-out of* PAUL *as a slightly younger man. He is wearing a suit, smiling broadly and making a 'thumbs up' gesture. They stand it upstage and contemplate it.* DAISY *finds it very amusing.*)

DAISY	What d'you think?
PAUL	Wow . . . (*He stares at it as if it is a very strange reflection. He is disconcerted.*)
DAISY	Graham found it in the store room at work.
GRAHAM	I wonder if Paul likes my present.
PAUL	Extraordinary.
EMMA	I expect he hates it.
DAISY	He saved it from recycling.
EMMA	Are you planning to do the kissing test? With Tammy?
PAUL	I wouldn't mind being recycled.
GRAHAM	No, that's been done.
PAUL	I've been trying to recycle myself.
GRAHAM	Maybe I'll take it one step further.

(EMMA *sighs and exits.*)

PAUL	But I've largely failed.

ACT ONE

GRAHAM I'd like to try it with you, actually. (*No response.*) Emma?

DAISY He also asked me to give you this. (*She hands him a bar of chocolate in a plain wrapper.*) They don't have the wrapper design yet.

PAUL It's a new product?

DAISY I think he wants you to work for him. (PAUL *stares.*) I mean, not for him. For the chocolate people.

PAUL I don't work for chocolate people. Only cardboard people.

DAISY Is that racist?

PAUL (*tries a bit of the chocolate*) He wants me to work for him?

DAISY He said you were good at advertising. And he wants to get some kind of happiness angle.

PAUL I can't do advertising anymore. Too depressing.

DAISY What d'you think? (PAUL *is chewing, frowning.*) I don't like it. It tastes like cheese.

PAUL Cheese?

DAISY Well, it's kind of creamy but, like ... sweaty or something, like cream that's gone cheesy. How long did you work with Graham?

PAUL Not long. I was trying to get out of advertising and he couldn't understand why. We didn't have

	much in common. But that's ten . . . maybe fifteen years ago.
DAISY	Was that when you had your breakdown?
PAUL	(*looks at her*) Um . . . I don't know if it was a breakdown . . . Is that what your Mother said?
DAISY	(*uncomfortable*) No, no. I don't think so. She doesn't talk about you. I mean, she doesn't, like, bitch about you.

(GRAHAM *is still tinkering with his laptop, fascinated by his own brain.*)

PAUL	It was a sort of . . . crisis, I suppose . . . I couldn't get a novel published, so . . . I didn't know what to do. Or who I was. If you know what I mean.
DAISY	'The world does not oblige'.
PAUL	(*beat, looks at her*) Exactly.
DAISY	So you wrote *How to be Happy*.
PAUL	Yeah, I did a bit of . . . self-help stuff. (*He contemplates the cut-out again.*) As my alter ego. Graham helped me with the marketing.

(GRAHAM *opens the face cream and sniffs it while studying his brain image.*)

DAISY	Mum said you were on telly.
PAUL	Yeah. Once or twice.
DAISY	(*smile*) That's so cool.
PAUL	They introduced me as Mr Happy.
DAISY	I tried to find you on You Tube.

PAUL	Oh, no. No chance.
DAISY	Are you coming to my show?
PAUL	Sure. Of course.
DAISY	We're doing *West Side Story* this year.
PAUL	Yeah, Mum told me. And you're playing . . .
DAISY	Anita. The Rita Moreno part. Lauren's playing Maria. She's amazing. She's going to try for *X Factor* next year. Oh, and she reads a lot. I told her about *Red Penguin*. You don't know when it's out?
PAUL	*Blue Penguin*.
DAISY	I mean, like, roughly.
PAUL	It's not exactly . . . a done deal yet.
	(*Noises off. Door opens and closes.*)
DAISY	Oh, I read *Suicide Hotel* again.
PAUL	Really?!
DAISY	I totally got it. I mean, like, understood it.
PAUL	It's not an easy read.
DAISY	You're an amazing writer.
PAUL	Oh, bless you.
	(KATY *enters with two bags of groceries. She lowers her bags onto the floor and takes off her overcoat. She is smiling but seems anxious, trying to gauge the mood.*)
KATY	Daisy! Hi!

DAISY	Hi, Katy. (*They kiss.* KATY *notices the cut-out.*)
KATY	Oh, my God! (*Beat.*) Look at that!
DAISY	It's Mr Happy. Graham found it in his store room.
KATY	(*laughs*) How amazing! Fantastic! (*Looks are exchanged between all three.*) How are you, anyway? Are you . . . ? It's great to see you!
DAISY	I'm cool. Yeah, I'm fine. I was just leaving, so . . .
KATY	(*face falls momentarily*) Oh, really? (*Smile.*) Okay, well . . .

(EMMA *enters and sees the opened face cream.*)

DAISY	Yeah, I better be going. Nice to . . .
EMMA	(*annoyed*) What are you doing?
KATY	Yes, lovely to see you.
GRAHAM	Sorry?
PAUL	Oh, here. (*Gives* DAISY *the 'get your baby to sleep' book.*)
EMMA	Why did you open it?
DAISY	Thanks. (*She leaves swiftly.*)
GRAHAM	What's the matter?
KATY	(*smiling incongruently*) Did I say something?
GRAHAM	I was just sniffing it.
KATY	She always rushes off. Ah, well . . . (*Begins tidying the room.*)

GRAHAM	Sometimes smell is very evocative.
PAUL	She was...
EMMA	Of what?
PAUL	...just leaving, so...
EMMA	Your ex-wife? I thought you were taking it back.
GRAHAM	Um...

(EMMA *sighs and exits.*)

KATY	You didn't tell her.
PAUL	No.
GRAHAM	(*irritated*) What's your problem?
PAUL	I'll wait 'til I talk to the new consultant. I want to give her a... complete picture, if you know what I mean.

(EMMA *enters.*)

EMMA	I hate those anti-ageing creams. You're in advertising! You should know about Polycollagen whatever. You should know that's pseudo-scientific bullshit.
PAUL	She's such a great girl.
GRAHAM	Well, I think they did studies with this one...
PAUL	So intelligent.
EMMA	What studies?
PAUL	Perceptive.
KATY	Yes.
EMMA	Did they give it to nuns?

GRAHAM	I'll stop buying you things.
KATY	Yes, she is.
GRAHAM	That's clearly the solution.
EMMA	They tested it on wrinkly nuns, did they? To see if they looked younger. To see if they were more kissable. (*She exits.*)
GRAHAM	Are you imagining that I bought it for you because you're wrinkly?
EMMA	(*pause, off:*) No! I just don't like wasting money! One hundred and twenty pounds for nothing!
KATY	What are we eating?

(KATY *collects the groceries and exits in the same direction as* EMMA. PAUL *sits next to* GRAHAM. *They sit, both thinking hard.*)

Scene Three

A moment later, it is evening. We hear Schubert's 'Winterreise' again.

> PAUL *sits in front of a box of photographs. He is working his way through them slowly.*

DAISY *is sprawled on the sofa, staring at the ceiling.* EMMA *enters, frowning.*

EMMA	What is this?
DAISY	(*beat*) Schubert. (EMMA *studies the CD case. The insert is blank with 'Schubert' and 'Winterreise' handwritten onto it.*)
EMMA	Did your father give you this? (*No response.*) Can you turn it down, please? (DAISY *sighs and*

uses a remote control to turn off the music.) What happened to Lady Gaga?

DAISY Oh, grow up.

(*Pause.*)

EMMA How was your father?

DAISY He doesn't want to work with Graham. He hates advertising.

EMMA (*beat*) Is that what he said?

DAISY I think I want to change my course.

EMMA (*sigh*) Daisy, I'm not going over and over this. I thought we agreed.

DAISY You and Graham agreed.

EMMA Oh, that's not true! That's not fair! You told me you'd gone off Psychology.

DAISY I want to do History. Or Politics.

EMMA What happened to Business Studies? History is hardly vocational, is it?

DAISY I don't want to work in an office. I want to do something that . . . makes a difference.

EMMA To what?

DAISY (*stares*) What d'you mean 'to what'? To the world.

EMMA You want to save the world?

DAISY Forget it.

EMMA Have you been talking to your father?

DAISY No.

(*Crying baby. The noise registers in* EMMA'S *face. But the crying soon stops.*)

(PAUL *has stopped looking at photographs. He is staring into space with a vacant expression.*)

EMMA   What about Katy? Did you talk to her?

DAISY   (*looks*) Why?

EMMA   I told you. She's a teacher.

DAISY   Nursery! She teaches babies!

EMMA   She's Deputy Head or something.

DAISY   Big deal. I don't like her, anyway. She's stuck up.

(EMMA *sighs heavily and walks towards the kitchen.*)

EMMA   I can't talk to you when you're like this.

DAISY   What's the matter?

(EMMA *turns.*)

EMMA   (*slight loss of temper*) Please can you try not to be so . . . judgemental?! So black and white about everything! (DAISY *stares.*) Life is tough! And people get through it, in their different ways, as best they can! The world isn't divided into good people and bad people!

(EMMA *exits. Beat.*)

DAISY   (*severely aggrieved*) I didn't mention good people and bad people! (*Beat.*) What's your problem?

(DAISY *picks up the remote control and presses a button. Schubert's 'Winterreise' continues. She turns the volume up. Extended pause.* EMMA *returns and sits.* DAISY *ignores her.*)

EMMA   I'm sorry. I'm just . . . exhausted at the moment. (*Beat.*) Please can you . . .

(DAISY *sighs and pauses the music again. Pause.* EMMA *is not sure what to say.*)

EMMA I'm so sorry, Daisy.

(PAUL *shuffles slowly out of the room, leaving the box on the floor.*)

EMMA Darling, I'm so sorry the way things turned out.

DAISY (*irritated*) Don't start that. For God's sake . . .

EMMA Well, it's true. And I'm always so scared it'll happen again. (DAISY *looks at her.*) I don't think I could cope . . .

DAISY D'you really think I'm bothered if you split up with Graham? (*Beat.*) It's not going to be like a total shock, you know?

(*They hold eye contact. Then* DAISY *looks away. Pause.*)

EMMA We're not going to split up.

(*Pause.* EMMA *doesn't know what else to say. She lifts herself wearily and moves towards the kitchen.*)

DAISY Anyway, she doesn't like you.

(EMMA *stops. Beat.*)

EMMA What d'you mean? (*Pause.*) How d'you know that? Did Dad tell you?

DAISY Don't tell him I told you!

EMMA No. I won't.

DAISY (*doesn't believe her*) Mum! You absolutely mustn't!

EMMA No! Of course I won't! Why would I?!

DAISY Anyway, it's not a surprise, is it? You're the ex-wife. Mother of his daughter. It's, like, obvious. (*Beat.*) Plus, she thinks you copy her.

EMMA What?

DAISY They've got the same sofa.

EMMA (*beat*) Well, it's similar..

DAISY It's the same. Exactly the same.

EMMA So what? Does she think we're all copying her? (DAISY *shrugs.*) Is she really that self-important?

DAISY Stuck-up.

EMMA (*beat*) No, not stuck-up.

DAISY Self-important is the definition of stuck-up. Don't you dare tell Dad, I'm serious.

EMMA Of course I won't.

Scene Four

PAUL has been inserting selected photographs into an album. EMMA is wearing a coat but begins removing it immediately.

EMMA Why did you tell Daisy that Katy doesn't like me?

(PAUL *looks up.* EMMA *hurls her coat onto a chair. Pause.* PAUL *slowly realises where this came from.*)

EMMA We have an agreement that Daisy is not exposed to any bitching, any negativity, about anybody!

PAUL	I know what it is. She misunderstood me. I made a comment about consumerism.
EMMA	What comment?
PAUL	People buying stuff they don't need, with money they don't have, to impress people they don't like.
EMMA	Who's buying stuff?
PAUL	Everyone. That's the point. It's a well-known... aphorism.
EMMA	I've never heard it. You also said you hate advertising.
PAUL	Christ, did she give you a transcript?
EMMA	It's not her fault.
PAUL	I didn't say I hate advertising.
EMMA	Don't tell her I told you.
PAUL	I said I didn't want to do it anymore.
EMMA	Paul, promise you won't tell her. (*He sighs.*) It's between you and me. She shouldn't be involved.
PAUL	Of course. (EMMA *glances occasionally at the photos.*)
EMMA	And promise you won't criticise Graham.
PAUL	I don't! I didn't!
EMMA	If you criticise advertising, you're criticising Graham.
PAUL	(*stares*) That's ridiculous. Just because that's his job...

EMMA	It's not just his job; it's his whole life.
PAUL	Advertising?! What d'you mean? Does he wear sandwich boards when you go out together? Does he carry a big sign pointing to a golf sale?
EMMA	You know, Graham has no hostility towards you. None at all.
PAUL	(*thrown, he frowns*) Why should he?
EMMA	You know what he said? The other day. He said "going forward, we should start trying to behave like an extended family". (PAUL *stares, grimacing.*) What? Don't you believe me? (*Beat.*) Those were his exact words.
PAUL	Really?
EMMA	Yes, really!
PAUL	He really used the expression 'going forward'?
	(*Beat.* EMMA *turns away and fetches her coat.*)
EMMA	I just can't talk to you.
	(EMMA *stands, coat in hand, wondering whether to leave.* PAUL *returns to his photos.*)
EMMA	Whatever words he used. He means it. He really does.
PAUL	(*dwindles into barely audible mumbling*) No, okay, that's . . . sure, that's an important, you know . . . agenda item . . . I'll add it to next month's –

EMMA (*re: one of the photos*) Is that Daisy?

(DAISY *enters, in the midst of a mobile phone (iPhone) call. She sits near* PAUL. *She is mostly listening but makes occasional noises of acknowledgement.*)

(PAUL *hands her the photo.* EMMA *puts her coat down. She smiles involuntarily, but briefly.*)

EMMA So cute.

GRAHAM (*off*) Daisy?

EMMA Did you give her that Schubert CD?
(PAUL *looks up.*)

(GRAHAM *enters.*)

GRAHAM Have you had breakfast?

(*No response. She continues listening to her caller, stony-faced.*)

EMMA There's a man singing; it's really depressing.

PAUL Oh, the 'Winterreise'. No, I burnt a copy for her.

EMMA You 'burnt' a copy?

PAUL Last time she broke up with Wayne.

DAISY Yeah, I miss you too, but . . .

EMMA It's really weird, a teenager listening to that. Or anyone, for that matter. You used to play it to annoy me, didn't you?

PAUL No, I didn't.

EMMA Now, she's playing it to annoy me.

GRAHAM	Daisy?
PAUL	It's about losing love. The journey into winter, and darkness.
EMMA	In German.
PAUL	She's good at German.

(GRAHAM *sighs and exits.*)

EMMA	Didn't you tell me it was recorded in Nazi Germany during the war?
PAUL	That particular recording, yes. Nineteen forty-three. It's Hans Hotter. But he wasn't a Nazi.
EMMA	And Schubert wrote the music when he was dying of syphilis at thirty-five.
PAUL	Thirty-one.
EMMA	Paul, it's suicide music!
DAISY	Yeah, I guess.
PAUL	No, it's not. I don't find it depressing. It's actually quite uplifting.
EMMA	(*glance at the Mr Happy cut-out*) I don't remember you recommending it in any of your happiness books.
PAUL	Well, it's uplifting if you're in a certain mood. It's a good break-up CD.
EMMA	It is not a break-up CD! Joni Mitchell, *Blue* is a break-up CD!
PAUL	If you say so.
EMMA	Or maybe Frank Sinatra, *Only the Lonely*.

PAUL	For some people it's a break-up CD.
EMMA	Like who? Like Eva Braun when she broke up with Hitler?
DAISY	Yeah, I do miss you. I told you that.
EMMA	I really hope to God she's broken up with that arsehole. You know he has a criminal record?
PAUL	(*shrug*) Young girls love bastards; that's a fact.
DAISY	It's just that you do my head in.
PAUL	But they grow out of it.
EMMA	How can you be so blasé?
PAUL	You blame me for it, don't you? Like everything else.
EMMA	No, I don't blame you. (*Beat.*) But we didn't provide a great . . . model for relationships. Did we?
PAUL	No. We didn't.
DAISY	I'm just . . . confused. I dunno.
PAUL	And we spoilt her, which, I notice you're continuing. She's now got a better car than . . . than most adults.
EMMA	Than you? Is that what you were going to say?
PAUL	No.
EMMA	Is that what bothers you?
PAUL	No, it isn't.

(GRAHAM *enters with a determined disposition.*)

GRAHAM   Daisy, can I please talk to you for a second?

DAISY   I'm on the phone.

GRAHAM   Yes. For the past half-an-hour.

(DAISY *sighs and leaves the room.*)

PAUL   There are studies which suggest, in spite of the . . . received wisdom, that people are happier before they have kids and after the kids leave home.

EMMA   Oh, that's nonsense.

PAUL   It's just the twenty years in between which are miserable.

EMMA   When your kids leave home, that's really tough. Haven't you heard of 'empty nest' syndrome?

GRAHAM   (*annoyed*) Daisy.

(PAUL *shrugs.*)

PAUL   You get over it. And then life is better.

EMMA   People don't have kids just to be happy.

PAUL   Don't they?

EMMA   No, they do it because it's part of life! It's one of the great experiences!

GRAHAM   Daisy! (*He leaves the room in pursuit.*)

EMMA   And you learn so much about yourself.

PAUL   Do you?

EMMA   (*taken aback*) Well, don't you think?!

PAUL   (*beat*) I'm not sure.

(EMMA *moves upstage, exasperated. She evaluates Mr Happy.*)

EMMA: I don't know why you keep going on about it. I mean, happiness. Haven't you learned your lesson?

PAUL: What d'you mean?

EMMA: I never bought into it, you know. I never thought it was really the point. To walk around for eighty years, grinning like an idiot.

PAUL: So, what is the point?

(*Pause.*)

EMMA: You don't want to work for Graham?

PAUL: Of course not.

(*He fetches the half-eaten chocolate bar and hands it to her.*)

PAUL: It's not fair-trade, is it?

EMMA: (*beat*) How should I know?

PAUL: Tell him, when he designs the wrapper, tell him not to forget the 'unfair trade' symbol. It's a little starving African baby.

(DAISY *returns to the room, still on the phone.*)

EMMA: Paul, for Christ's sake . . . We're trying to do you a favour.

DAISY: Yeah, I guess so.

PAUL: Crumbs from the table.

EMMA: (*prepares to leave*) Oh, fine! All right! If that's your attitude!

(She puts her coat on too quickly, has to remove it and put it on again. PAUL watches.)

DAISY   You're a bastard to me sometimes.

EMMA   Crumbs from the table! Jesus! You see how negative you are!

DAISY   You know you are.

PAUL   Well, that's what it is, isn't it?

EMMA   No, it's not! It's a genuine offer! You were good at advertising! Graham rates you very highly!

DAISY   What's that music? What are you listening to?

EMMA   You know, I went to such trouble not to criticise you in front of Daisy. I really went out of my way. A lot of women don't do that.

PAUL   It was a struggle, was it?

EMMA   Yes, it was. Because you behaved like a complete shit!

PAUL   Well, I'll be out of your way, soon, so . . .

(This stops EMMA from leaving.)

DAISY   I'm trying to get into classical.

EMMA   What d'you mean? You're not moving?

PAUL   I have cancer.

DAISY   D'you like Schubert?

PAUL   Lung cancer.

	(*Pause.* EMMA *stares, frozen. Her coat is half on.*)
DAISY	(*frown*) No, Schubert. He's a composer.
EMMA	Does Daisy know?
PAUL	No.
EMMA	Lung cancer!?
PAUL	Also in the lymph glands.
DAISY	Why would I ask if you like sherbet?
EMMA	(*crushed*) Oh, God . . . (*Pause.*) Why didn't you tell me? (*Beat.*) Before we started arguing.
PAUL	I didn't intend to tell you.
DAISY	I love sherbet lemons.
EMMA	It's like you provoke me into saying something horrible and that's the moment you choose . . .
PAUL	Why is everything about you?
EMMA	(*beat*) Are you having chemotherapy?
PAUL	(*beat*) I don't think so. I'm seeing another consultant next week.
DAISY	Have you heard of Sherbet Dip Dab?
	(EMMA *sits, then glances at the photos in front of her.*)
DAISY	No, for real. Sherbet Dip Dab.
PAUL	I thought I might do an album for Daisy. For her birthday.
	(EMMA *picks up a photo.*)

DAISY	Yeah, it's like a lollipop thing. You dip it in sherbet.
EMMA	How old are you here?
DAISY	My Dad used to buy them when he was a boy.
PAUL	I don't know. Ten, eleven . . .
DAISY	You can still get them.

(EMMA *holds back tears, which takes some effort.* PAUL *is secretly pleased at her reaction.*)

DAISY	Well, what d'you think it was? (*Smile.*) Did you think it was a composer?
PAUL	To be honest . . .
DAISY	(*enjoying herself*) Sherbet Dipdab. Seventeen, ninety-three to eighteen . . . (*Wayne cuts her off.*)
PAUL	I didn't think you'd take it so badly.
EMMA	(*looks at him*) Oh, Jesus, Paul!
PAUL	Sorry.
DAISY	No, I'm not making fun.
EMMA	Apart from anything else . . . This will destroy Daisy.

(PAUL *is hurt, irritated.*)

DAISY	(*sigh*) Wayne, don't be . . .
EMMA	She's been through so much already. And her eighteenth birthday next week. This'll hit her for six. I know it will.

(*Wayne has hung up.* DAISY *discards the phone and sighs heavily.*)

EMMA	(*a thought occurs*) You know, her show's coming up. *West Side Story*.
PAUL	Yes, I know.
EMMA	(*genuinely concerned*) She's been so excited about it. (*Beat.*) Maybe you shouldn't tell her . . . Until after the performance. She's desperate for us all to be there.
PAUL	Well, if I die in the meantime, you can take that instead. (*The cardboard cut-out.*) Just stick it in my seat; she won't notice.
EMMA	(*tinge of dread*) You're not going to die, Paul. Are you? (*Extended uncomfortable pause.* EMMA *doesn't know what to say.*) I'm sorry. I better go.

(*She exits swiftly. Pause.*)

PAUL	(*to himself*) 'Going forward.' Christ almighty . . .

(PAUL *stands in front of the cut-out and stares into its eyes for a moment. Then he lifts it and carries it out of the room.*)

Scene Five

Night. EMMA *is sitting on sofa, depressed, exhausted. She is half-dressed.*

PAUL *enters and sits next to her.*

GRAHAM *enters, wearing a dressing gown. She looks at his face, then down at his bare legs.*

EMMA	I'm not really in the mood.

GRAHAM	That's okay.
EMMA	Paul has cancer.
GRAHAM	(*beat*) What?!

(KATY *enters, stands behind* PAUL. *He takes her hand.*)

KATY	Did you tell her?
GRAHAM	Are you serious?
PAUL	Yes.
EMMA	Lung cancer.
GRAHAM	Christ.
PAUL	She was worried about Daisy.
KATY	(*beat*) Right.
EMMA	I need to make peace with him. For Daisy. (*Beat.*) It's not as if I haven't been trying. I mean, I think it's over, that I'm over it and then he says something stupid to Daisy and I'm hooked back in. (*Big sigh.*) But, that's it, I can't fight with him anymore. It's too exhausting anyhow.
GRAHAM	(*still digesting the news*) Is it serious?
KATY	You okay?
EMMA	(*she looks*) It's lung cancer.
GRAHAM	I mean, is it terminal?
PAUL	Graham offered me some work.
EMMA	I think so.
PAUL	Via Daisy.
KATY	Really?
PAUL	New chocolate campaign.

EMMA	I need to make friends with him.
KATY	Crumbs from the table.
GRAHAM	Well, we're doing our best.
PAUL	No, I don't think so.
GRAHAM	Aren't we?
PAUL	I was good at advertising.
KATY	Oh, I know. I didn't mean it like that.

(*No answer from* EMMA.)

GRAHAM	Don't you think? We're offering him work.
EMMA	That's just crumbs from the table.
GRAHAM	Sure, but they need the money, don't they? You'd think he'd be grateful.
PAUL	They have the same sofa.
KATY	What?

(GRAHAM *paces*.)

PAUL	Exactly the same.
KATY	Are they copying us?
PAUL	Daisy told me. It's in their 'snug', whatever that is.
KATY	Snug. It's a small, cosy living space.
GRAHAM	We've gone out of our way. We moved here so Daisy would be closer. I mean, that's a big sacrifice.
EMMA	Is it?
GRAHAM	Yeah, it is! I was very happy where I was.
PAUL	Graham loves living right next to us.

EMMA	(*frown*) Really?
PAUL	In a bigger house.
GRAHAM	He's jealous of us, isn't he?
KATY	Really?
EMMA	Oh, sure.
PAUL	Of course. It's the biggest, best house in the area.
EMMA	He's got a huge chip on his shoulder.
KATY	(*shrug*) Personally, I prefer our house.

(*Baby crying.* EMMA *sighs heavily.* GRAHAM *exits.*)

PAUL   They asked a group of Harvard students to choose between two scenarios – one in which you earn fifty thousand dollars a year and everyone else earns twenty-five – and another in which you earn a hundred thousand but everyone else earns two hundred and fifty thousand. (*Beat.*) Most people went for the first option.

KATY   What d'you expect from Harvard students?

PAUL   There are other studies. Having more money is not as important as having more than others.

(EMMA *begins crying.*)

KATY   I don't understand the copying. I mean, it's not the first time, is it? You'd think they'd want to be different.

PAUL   Nobody's different. It's not about being different. (*Beat.*) It's about being the same, only better. (*Beat.*) Richer and bigger and better.

KATY   I'm really tired. (*She moves towards the door.*)

(GRAHAM *returns and finds* EMMA *crying. His face falls. Pause.*)

GRAHAM   What's the matter?

PAUL   But they're missing the point.

EMMA   I feel so . . . lost . . . So tired . . .

GRAHAM   (*weary*) Come to bed.

PAUL   It's so clear to me now.

GRAHAM   (*pause*) Geoff in accounts has been on Prozac for ten years. He swears by it.

EMMA   (*beat, no reaction*) Go to bed.

KATY   Are you coming?

(*Pause.* GRAHAM *wants to go to bed but feels he should stay with* EMMA.)

(KATY *exits.*)

GRAHAM   I have a breakfast meeting.

EMMA   I said go to bed.

PAUL   Why does it have to take something like this?

EMMA   Who with?

(PAUL *turns to find* KATY *has gone. Pause.*)

EMMA   D'you like this Tammy girl?

GRAHAM	(*beat*) How d'you mean?
EMMA	I guess she's younger. Less wrinkly, isn't she?
GRAHAM	You're not wrinkly.
EMMA	(*matter-of-fact*) You said I was.
GRAHAM	(*beat*) What?! No, I didn't.
EMMA	You said, "are you thinking I bought the cream for you because you're wrinkly".
GRAHAM	(*beat*) I didn't say that.
EMMA	Yes, you did.
GRAHAM	(*long-suffering sigh*) I said, "because you think I'm wrinkly". (EMMA *frowns.*) I mean, "because you think I think you're wrinkly". I don't know what I said but I don't think you're wrinkly, I most certainly don't.
EMMA	Doesn't matter. (*She is staring, scrutinising.*) Do you like this Tammy girl?
GRAHAM	(*beat, shrug*) I have no specific opinion . . .

(PAUL *shuffles out of the room.*)

EMMA	How come I never know what you're thinking? What you're feeling? (*Beat.*) I mean, what you're really feeling.
GRAHAM	(*beat, shrug*) Do people really know what they're really feeling?
EMMA	I'm not asking you to take the Pepsi Cola test. I just want you to talk a bit more. About how you feel.
GRAHAM	I feel very tired. (*Beat.*) And I'm going to bed.
EMMA	I thought you wanted to make love.

ACT ONE

GRAHAM Tomorrow. Maybe. (EMMA *looks away finally, stares into space.*) Actually . . . at some point . . . I'd like to do it with the cap. (EMMA, *distracted, does not respond.*) Em?

EMMA Right. Okay.

(*Beat.* GRAHAM *leaves. Darkness slowly falls. We hear the beginning of Mozart's Mass in C Minor.*)

Scene Six

After about a minute of Mozart's Mass in darkness, the lights begin to rise into morning.

> PAUL *paces in and out. He is on the phone. He is exhilarated, bewildered, experiencing a range of emotions.*

PAUL I've never heard of sarcoidosis. (*Pause.*) Right. (*Beat.*) Right. (*Beat.*) But it's not cancer. (*Beat.*) Fuck. (*Pause.*) Yes, I'm very angry. How could this happen?! I mean . . . (*Pause.*) Right. (*Pause. He checks his watch.*) I'm not sure. Maybe later. I'll call you. 'Bye.

> (PAUL *hangs up and stands, frozen, thoughts whirling through his brain.*)

(EMMA *marches into the room, and out the other side, with an armful of clothes.*)

GRAHAM (*off*) Emma?

> (KATY *wanders into the room with a cup of tea and a biscuit.*)

PAUL (*mind racing*) They fucked up. They misdiagnosed. (*Beat.*) Lung cancer

	notoriously difficult, apparently. (*Stares at the phone.*) Jesus, I'll sue the fuckers. How could they do this to me?
KATY	What?
PAUL	(*stares at her, tries to take it in*) I don't have cancer. (*Beat.*) I have sarcoidosis.
GRAHAM	(*off*) Em?
PAUL	(*beat*) Which is not great. But it's not cancer.
GRAHAM	(*off*) Are you coming?
KATY	(*pause*) Are you serious?
PAUL	Completely.

(KATY *stares, then looks away, trying to process this information. Almost unconsciously, she takes another bite of her biscuit.*)

| KATY | Wow. I can't believe it. |
| PAUL | Me neither. |

(EMMA *enters, without the clothes, but with a diaphragm in a plastic container. She perches on the sofa for a moment's rest and contemplation.*)

| KATY | Are they sure? |
| PAUL | Apparently. |

(*Pause.* KATY *hugs* PAUL. *She cries briefly.*)

| PAUL | Lets go out. I want to go somewhere. |
| GRAHAM | (*off*) Emma? |

PAUL	Luigi's.
KATY	Really?
PAUL	(*checks watch*) It's eleven. We could have a . . . champagne breakfast or something.
KATY	Right now?
PAUL	Yeah, right now.
KATY	Okay, hold on.

(*She exits hurriedly.* PAUL *stands, thinking for a few moments. Then he uses a remote control to move the CD onto the 'Gloria' of the C Minor Mass. He turns up the volume and celebrates like a footballer who has scored a goal.*)

(GRAHAM *enters carrying laptop and wearing EEG cap, shirt, underpants and socks – no trousers.* EMMA *stares at him.*)

(*After performing a little dance to the 'Gloria' and bouncing on the sofa,* PAUL *switches the music off and exits swiftly.*)

GRAHAM	(*mildly irritated*) What are you doing?
EMMA	What am I doing?
GRAHAM	Are you ready?
EMMA	I thought you meant, do it with this cap. (*Holds up diaphragm container.*)

(*Pause. They stare.*)

GRAHAM	We haven't used that for ages.

EMMA   Why have you got it on already?

GRAHAM   Because . . . It takes a lot of doing. I can't do this in the middle.

EMMA   So, you're not bothered about this? (*The diaphragm.*)

GRAHAM   We can use a condom.

EMMA   (*beat*) You haven't got that on as well, have you? (GRAHAM *stares.*) Is it an ordinary condom or an electro condom?

             (DAISY *enters and immediately senses she shouldn't be there.*)

EMMA   I thought you'd gone.

             (GRAHAM *exits to the kitchen.* DAISY *sees the diaphragm.*)

DAISY   Oh, my God.

             (*She exits.* EMMA *lowers her head into her hands.*)

             (PAUL *enters, ready to leave.*)

PAUL   (*as he enters*) I'm just going to call Emma. In case she tells Daisy.

KATY   (*off*) Okay.

             (PAUL *dials a number.*)

             (EMMA'S *mobile phone rings. She is disturbed by the ring tone. [NB: The tune is 'Be My Baby' by the Ronettes.]*)

EMMA   Hello?

PAUL   Hi. It's me. I'm okay.

EMMA   Sorry?

PAUL	It was a misdiagnosis. (*Beat.*) I have sarcoidosis, not cancer. So . . . I'm okay. I mean it's not . . . terminal, or anything.
EMMA	Are you serious?
PAUL	Yeah.
EMMA	They misdiagnosed? How could they do that?
PAUL	(*deep breath*) God knows. You didn't say anything to Daisy?
EMMA	No! No, of course.
PAUL	Right. Good.
EMMA	No, of course not. (*Pause.*) Wow. Paul, that's . . . (*Beat.*) That's great. That's really . . . fantastic news.
PAUL	Thanks. (*Pause.*) I'll catch you later.
EMMA	Okay. (*Pause.*) Okay, 'bye.
PAUL	'Bye.

(PAUL *sits.*)

(EMMA *sits also and takes in the news. Suddenly she heaves a huge sigh of relief. She begins to cry but stops herself.* GRAHAM *enters.*)

GRAHAM	Are we doing this or . . . ?
EMMA	No. (*Beat.*) No, sorry. Go and . . . have a wank. (*Beat.*) Wouldn't that be much the same? In terms of brain buzz?
GRAHAM	No, it's not the same. (*Beat.*) Call me old-fashioned, but I'd have thought that making love to your wife is a more emotional experience than masturbation.

EMMA	Not when your husband's dressed as an android. (GRAHAM *stares*.) Sorry, I'm not doing it. Anyway, I have a mild fear of electrocution. Paul's okay.

(KATY *enters, wearing shoes and overcoat*.)

GRAHAM	What?
KATY	Are we going?
EMMA	He just called.
PAUL	Yes, sorry.
EMMA	It was a misdiagnosis. He doesn't have cancer.

(*Doorbell*.)

KATY	Who's that? (*She exits to answer the door*.)
GRAHAM	Seriously?

(PAUL *exits also*.)

EMMA	I'll do it without the electro cap if you like.
GRAHAM	(*beat*) How could they misdiagnose?

(EMMA *shrugs*.)

(DAISY *enters, out of breath and in an agitated state*.)

DAISY	I can't talk about it. It's too gross.

(*She sits on the sofa and covers her face with her hands*.)

PAUL	(*enters*) What? What's the matter?

(GRAHAM *wanders out of the room*. EMMA *remains sitting, thinking*.)

	(KATY *enters.*)
DAISY	No, I can't talk about it.
	(PAUL *indicates to* KATY *to give them a moment.* KATY *exits.* DAISY *gets up and paces around the room.*)
DAISY	I like walk in and they're about to . . . do it . . . And he's got this . . . thing on his head . . .
PAUL	(*grimacing*) What thing?
DAISY	This . . . cap with, like, wires sticking out of it, like a robot. It's so totally gross! (*Beat.* PAUL *is frozen, grimacing.*) I can't live there anymore. I'm moving out.
PAUL	(*pulling himself together*) Daisy, listen . . .
DAISY	You don't know what it's like! They're both miserable, bickering all the time! And Jack keeps everyone awake all night!
PAUL	Did you give them the book?
DAISY	What book?

(EMMA *raises herself with some effort and exits.*)

PAUL	I gave you a book. *How to get your Child to Sleep.*
DAISY	I forgot.
PAUL	(*slightly irritated*) Well, it would really help them.
DAISY	I don't want to help them! I want them to break up!

PAUL	(*beat*) You don't mean that.
DAISY	Oh, yes, I do!
PAUL	Listen, we were just going out . . .
DAISY	(*annoyed*) Oh, right. Pardon me. (*She moves to leave.*)
PAUL	Just give them the book. Actually, it might break them up quicker.
DAISY	(*looks*) How come?
PAUL	Well, they're so busy, so stressed all the time. If it's all some kind of...unconscious avoidance strategy . . . (DAISY *stares blankly.*) Sometimes people over-complicate their lives to avoid things. You know? (*Pause.* DAISY *is still staring.* PAUL *shrugs.*) If there are deep-seated . . . marital problems, then . . . (DAISY *thinks hard.*) Listen, by the way, it's not a big deal, but, if we have a private conversation . . . I really don't want your mother to hear about it.
DAISY	Like what?
PAUL	Like, never mind, just . . . (*He politely ushers her towards the door.*)
DAISY	She told you?!
PAUL	Let's go.

Scene Seven

Day. PAUL, *alone on stage. He seems uptight, edgy and is studying the sofa on which he is sitting. Then he picks up 'The Times' from the coffee table.* EMMA *walks through the room quickly with a couple of toys. They don't look at each other. Finally:*

PAUL   You read *The Times* now?

EMMA   (*off*) Occasionally. (*Beat.*) Why? What do you read?

PAUL   I don't read newspapers. Too depressing. It's like paying someone to kick you in the balls on a daily basis.

(*He discards the newspaper, then picks up a fashion magazine. He flicks through it with an expression of disgust.*)

PAUL   Christ almighty ...

(EMMA *enters with an armful of toys and walks back across the stage.*)

PAUL   Is this yours?

EMMA   (*as she exits*) No, it's Daisy's.

(PAUL *is appalled.*)

PAUL   You're joking? She's reading this shit? (*Flicks through it more quickly.*) It's full of emaciated young girls!

(EMMA *returns to the room, still carrying the toys.*)

EMMA   As I've said many times, if you have a problem, you talk to her. I'm not doing 'good cop, bad cop' anymore.

(EMMA *exits again.*)

(*Doorbell.*)

PAUL   It wasn't really like that.

EMMA   (*off*) They're not all emaciated. And she likes clothes. What's wrong with liking clothes?

(KATY *enters and walks through the room.*)

PAUL I hate the fashion industry. They're trying to turn us into a nation of narcissists who have to stay 'on trend' by throwing away everything we bought from sweatshops last year.

EMMA (*off*) You're fast becoming a grumpy old bugger. I bet Katy likes fashion.

PAUL (*beat*) No. She's stylish. Not fashionable.

(KATY *enters with* GRAHAM.)

EMMA (*off*) Yeah, right.

KATY Come in, come in.

GRAHAM Oh, wow, this is nice.

PAUL She doesn't waste money buying the latest crap.

KATY It's sort of . . . bijou, but . . .

EMMA (*off*) She can't afford to.

GRAHAM We have the same sofa. I think.

KATY Oh, really? Wow. Well, it's a nice sofa.

PAUL (*annoyed*) Well, you're so lucky to be able to . . . wallow in so much cash. Where is Graham anyway?

GRAHAM I haven't been here for awhile.

EMMA (*off*) No idea.

KATY Haven't you? No, I suppose not.

(EMMA *enters with no toys.*)

EMMA Paul, can I ask what you want?

KATY	Shall I give you the tour?
GRAHAM	Oh.
EMMA	I haven't really got time.
GRAHAM	Okay.
EMMA	As per usual.
KATY	(*smile*) It won't take long.
PAUL	Well, it's not easy . . .
GRAHAM	No, that'd be great.
PAUL	It's a delicate matter.
KATY	The kitchen's through here.
EMMA	(*sigh*) Did Daisy say something? (PAUL *stares*.)
KATY	(*as they exit*) We had new units put in.
EMMA	I knew it! Bloody typical!
PAUL	She was pretty disturbed!
EMMA	Get out. (*Beat*.) Just get out. I'm not talking to you.
PAUL	It's not healthy to walk in on your mother in the middle of a . . . weird fantasy sex game.
EMMA	What?! (*Beat*.) What did she tell you, exactly?
PAUL	Very little! But enough to get the idea.
EMMA	What idea?
PAUL	Well, I assume Graham was . . . C-3PO or something . . . And you're Princess Leia commanding him to bend you over the Imperial sofa . . .
EMMA	If that turns you on . . .

PAUL   You know very well that I'm not into that kind of bullshit.

EMMA   No, I know exactly how ... unimaginative you are. He was wearing an electro ... EEG cap which measures ... brain waves or something. It's the new thing in advertising. Someone did brain scans on people kissing and then eating chocolate to see which was more exciting. He wanted to take it ... to the next level.

(*Pause.* PAUL *is staring, frowning severely.*)

PAUL   This cap is ... plugged in somewhere?

EMMA   (*wearily*) Yes. And it's attached to a laptop. You can see a brain image. Actually, it's quite interesting.

PAUL   Does he really think his ... cheesy chocolate is more exciting than sex?

EMMA   (*sigh*) No, I don't think so.

PAUL   You don't *think* so? (EMMA *exits.*) Christ, I feel sorry for you.

EMMA   (*off*) Well, don't.

(KATY *enters, followed by* GRAHAM.)

KATY   We rented one of those ... you know, floor sanders.

GRAHAM   Oh, right.

EMMA   (*off*) In fact, he's got a pretty high sex drive.

(PAUL *grimaces severely.*)

GRAHAM   Our floorboards are ... quite similar ...

(KATY *leads* GRAHAM *out again.*)

PAUL You mean, normally? Or just when he's plugged into the mains? (PAUL, *in a very bad mood, prepares to leave.*) Anyway, it's been a pleasure . . .

(EMMA *enters.*)

EMMA Did Daisy tell you about her placement?

PAUL (*beat*) No.

EMMA (*sigh*) She never tells you anything important. Um . . . It looks like she's got an intern placement during her gap year. (*Beat.*) At an agency.

PAUL I thought she wanted to do voluntary work. What d'you mean 'an agency'? Advertising? (EMMA *stares.* PAUL *is angry.*) She's not doing advertising! I'd rather she spent the year . . . lap-dancing in Thailand!

EMMA When are you going to get over it?

PAUL (*beat*) What?

EMMA The fact that I married an advertising guru.

PAUL Oh, is he officially a guru now? Does he wear robes?

EMMA He's keeping the economy going.

PAUL Single-handed?

EMMA (*over*) Unlike some people.

PAUL Yeah, because that's why we're here, isn't it? To keep the economy going. Like we're all . . . worker ants or something..

EMMA Somebody has to, don't they? Somebody has to create wealth, create jobs . . .

PAUL Is that what he's doing?

EMMA	Jobs depend, don't they, on people buying products. And advertising is telling people about products.
PAUL	No, it's not, it's convincing people that they need stuff they didn't even know they wanted!
EMMA	To impress people they don't like.
PAUL	Exactly! Four hundred billion a year is spent creating perpetual dissatisfaction!
EMMA	Listen to you with your hi-fi and all your gadgets . . .
PAUL	Yes, I'm a victim too!
EMMA	You're worse than anyone.
PAUL	We're all victims! We're powerless to resist!
EMMA	I'm not a victim. Sometimes I buy things; sometimes I don't. I like having choices.
PAUL	(*messianic*) Big business has taken over. You don't understand. We used to be citizens in this country. That's something to be. But a consumer – which is what we are now – that's bullshit! There's no community anymore!
EMMA	Yes, there is.
PAUL	(*over*) The only thing we do together is shuffle around like zombies . . .
EMMA	Glad you're including yourself.
PAUL	(*over*) . . . in vast shopping malls resembling cathedrals, all looking for the perfect fucking sofa! The rest of the time we sit in our little houses watching endless adverts and cooking programmes and celebrity crap and 'how to look young' and news! (EMMA *sighs and exits. Noises off:* EMMA *unloading the dishwasher with some aggression.*) Never-ending, twenty-four hour fucking news about how many more of our boys

have died in the Middle East and hardly ever a mention of how many fucking Arabs we've killed or the fact that we're over there for oil to keep Big Business going!

EMMA (*off*) It's not just about oil . . .

PAUL Oh, sorry! I forgot! We're over there to protect our freedoms, to protect our right to watch crap TV all the time and waste all our money on consumer bullshit!

EMMA (*off*) It's partly about terrorism. But, never mind.

PAUL Yeah, exactly. Protect our freedoms. We have to bomb people to stop them bombing us. Makes perfect sense.

EMMA (*off*) You'd prefer life under the Taliban, would you? With no freedom at all. Or maybe you'd prefer Chairman Mao. You'd like us all to wear those little tunics.

PAUL Yeah, terrific.

(EMMA *enters, determined, with plate and tea towel.*)

EMMA No, actually, you wouldn't, would you? You'd hate Communism. And you'd hate Islamism.

PAUL No shit.

EMMA Because you know what the truth is?

PAUL No idea. Tell me.

EMMA You know what would happen? If you were appointed world . . . emperor or something.

PAUL World emperor?

EMMA You'd lock yourself away in your big office. You'd put on some of your miserable music. And you'd sit down to design your . . . perfect utopia. And you know what would happen?

PAUL	I'm all ears.
EMMA	You'd spend ages going all around the houses and, in the end, you'd come right back to consumer capitalism because you couldn't do without your fucking iPhone!
PAUL	Brilliant.
EMMA	I know you too well, Paul. It's miserablism; that's all it is. Its misanthropy and resentment and bitterness disguised as political conviction. Now, if you'll excuse me, I have housework to do.

(*She exits.*)

PAUL	You've really given that some thought, haven't you?
EMMA	(*off, beat*) No, not really.

(*She returns.*)

EMMA	Well, yes, I have actually. Because it bothers me. It bugs me. I'm fed up of feeling judged by you.
PAUL	That's not my intention. If you feel judged, that's your business.
EMMA	(*snorts dismissively*) Yeah, right.

(*She exits.*)

PAUL	Yeah, right. You're starting to sound like your daughter.

(*Pause. More banging and crashing from the kitchen.*)

PAUL	Well, I apologise for having a go at consumer capitalism, but it is destroying the planet, so . . .
EMMA	(*off*) You're an environmentalist now, are you?

PAUL	Yes. An environmentalist and a miserablist. They tend to go together . . .
EMMA	(*off*) I bet I know more about climate change than you do!
PAUL	Oh, really?
EMMA	(*off*) Graham's been looking into solar panels. Have you done that?
PAUL	Never mind solar panels, he should give up advertising!

(*Enters with tea towel and some cutlery.*)

EMMA	It's just a coincidence, is it? That you've developed these views . . .
PAUL	I haven't developed these views . . .
EMMA	(*over*) . . . since me and Graham . . .
PAUL	(*over*) I know about consumer culture. Because I know about unhappiness.
EMMA	Yeah, you were like an advertising man, selling happiness.
PAUL	It's better than selling thirty different types of shampoo!
EMMA	No, it isn't! Because it's a big lie! Life is not about happiness!

(*Beat.*)

PAUL	Well, it shouldn't be about misery.
EMMA	Who's miserable?
PAUL	We all are! We're all getting richer and richer and more miserable.
EMMA	No, we're not.

PAUL	There are studies. You look at the studies.
EMMA	(*increasing volume*) These days, there's a huge 'self-help', psychology industry measuring, categorising people. Everyone's got a syndrome. Everyone thinks 'if I'm not happy, there's something wrong with me'. No, there's nothing wrong with you! You're a human being! A human being is not a happy bunny!

(*She exits.* PAUL *is left to digest this.*)

(GRAHAM *enters, followed by* KATY.)

GRAHAM	But I'm sure we'll be okay.
KATY	Yes.
GRAHAM	Ultimately.

(EMMA *returns.*)

EMMA	Weren't you leaving?
GRAHAM	We just need some quality time. I mean, we barely get time to talk!
KATY	Sure.

(EMMA'S *mobile phone rings. Once again, the 'Be My Baby' ring tone.*)

GRAHAM	So, we're not really . . . connected.
EMMA	God, I hate this tune.
KATY	Well, communication is crucial.
GRAHAM	Yes. (*Thinks.*)
EMMA	If this is an estate agent . . .
GRAHAM	I thought I was good at that. But . . .
EMMA	They keep calling me for some reason.

GRAHAM	Maybe not.
EMMA	(*answers the phone*) Hello? (*She exits to the kitchen.*)
GRAHAM	The other night . . . she told me she never knows what I'm feeling.
KATY	Oh, really?
EMMA	(*off*) No. No.

(GRAHAM *shrugs, wearily.*)

KATY	Well . . . There's an easy solution.
GRAHAM	Yes. Just tell her, right? (*They smile.*)
EMMA	(*off*) How did you get this number?
GRAHAM	Doesn't sound so bad . . . Anyway, if you could just mention to Paul . . .
KATY	Yes, sure.
EMMA	(*off*) No, thank you.
GRAHAM	I'd love him to participate. And it's right up his street. We want to make a connection, in the consumer's mind, between our chocolate bar and the deep-seated desire for pleasure, you know?
KATY	Right.
GRAHAM	So, at this stage, we're just brainstorming notions of pleasure, happiness, where it comes from, what it means . . . Then we want to create metaphors, images which will . . . tap into that yearning, if you follow me.
KATY	Yes.

PAUL	'Be My Baby'?
KATY	I think I do.
EMMA	(*in the doorway*) What?
GRAHAM	Well, anyway . . .
PAUL	Your ring tone.
GRAHAM	. . . it's a lovely house.
PAUL	It's 'Be My Baby'.
KATY	Well, we like it.
PAUL	The Ronettes.
GRAHAM	And it's great to see you.
EMMA	Is it?
KATY	Yes! You too!
EMMA	Whatever it is I really hate it.
	(*She follows* GRAHAM *out of the room.*)
KATY	(*as she goes*) I'll see you soon, I'm sure.
PAUL	Why? Because it's our song?
EMMA	(*beat*) Our song?
PAUL	Don't you remember Crete?
EMMA	(*pause*) That was a long time ago.
PAUL	Daisy's birthday this week. So it's eighteen years and nine months.
EMMA	It's hardly 'our song'.

PAUL	You told me the lyrics perfectly summed up your feelings.
EMMA	(*beat*) I was probably drunk. Too much Ouzo. (*She begins pushing buttons on the phone.*) I don't know how it got on here. (*A thought occurs.*) You didn't do it, did you?
PAUL	(*frown*) Why would I? (*Pause.*) Don't you know how to change it? (PAUL *takes the phone.*)
EMMA	No. (*She watches him pushing buttons.*) I can make a call; that's about it.
PAUL	Here. If you want, you can have different ring tones for different people.
EMMA	Oh, right. (*Beat.*) Maybe I'll get a Schubert ring tone for you. (*Beat.*) So every time you call, I'll hear this . . . syphilitic dirge.

(*He stares at her. Pause.*)

EMMA	What? Have you done it?
PAUL	(*matter-of-fact*) I think about it a lot, you know. That holiday. (*Pause.*) That little car with its headlights held on with tape. Don't you remember? (*Pause.*) We found a Sixties CD in that gift shop because we didn't want to listen to Greek music anymore. And we played it over and over – especially 'Be My Baby' – and sang along, as we drove around, finding little coves . . .
EMMA	What's your point?
PAUL	I know you're determined to hate me.
EMMA	I don't hate you.
PAUL	But this idea that everything went wrong because of my affair . . .
EMMA	I haven't got time for this. (*She exits to the kitchen.*)

PAUL	You don't know how hard you are to live with!
EMMA	(*off*) Oh, fine, yeah, it's all my fault!
PAUL	I'm not saying that! I'm saying things go wrong! People have problems! It's tough! Relationships are not like they are in the coffee adverts!
EMMA	(*off*) You don't say!
PAUL	You always wanted it fairy-tale, perfect, like we're meant for each other, or something.
EMMA	(*enters*) What's wrong with thinking you're meant for someone?!
PAUL	It's not real! Who you end up with is . . . largely random!
EMMA	God, you're so romantic.
PAUL	Listen, I love a bit of romance.
EMMA	Since when?
PAUL	But you don't take it too fucking seriously.
EMMA	I really don't have time for this bullshit.
PAUL	Right. Okay. (*He moves to the door.*)
EMMA	Listen, I'm concerned about Daisy. She's confused at the moment. But if she decides to do business studies . . . Even, God help us, advertising. She's all grown up. Please will you let her do what she wants?
PAUL	Of course I will.

(*Pause.* PAUL *is staring, scrutinising. She holds his gaze.*)

EMMA	I don't hate you. I don't blame you. (*Beat.*) I realised something. Blaming just keeps you

hooked in. You can't detach if you keep blaming. Or hating. So I don't. I really don't.

(*Pause.*)

PAUL   You've detached, have you?

EMMA   Yes. I have.

Scene Eight

Evening. 'Der Leiermann' from Schubert's 'Winterreise' is playing. PAUL *is slouched on the sofa, frowning and tapping numbers into the calculator application on his iPhone.*

After a few moments, EMMA *wanders in, yawning, rubbing her neck. She sits right next to* PAUL *on the sofa. They both stare into space for a moment.*

Then PAUL *gets up and begins pacing deliberately from one side of the room to the other.*

GRAHAM *enters, eating chocolate. Pause.*

GRAHAM   Does Paul want to do it? (*Pause.*) The chocolate thing?

EMMA   Don't think so.

(*Pause.* GRAHAM *sits.*)

(*On his first attempt,* PAUL'S *steps were too short so he tries again, lengthening his stride so he can cross the room in ten steps.*)

GRAHAM   We might ditch it anyway. The happiness angle. (*Beat.*) We're not sure the chocolate is good enough. (*Takes another bite.*) Maybe it's for kids. (*Beat.*) Go for the path of least resistance.

	(*Concentrates on the taste, frowning.*) Maybe we can make it cool. (*Beat.*) Maybe it's for tweens.
EMMA	What the hell are tweens?
GRAHAM	Eight to twelve.
	(KATY *enters, carrying the Mr Happy cut-out.* PAUL *stops his pacing.*)
KATY	I don't want this in the toilet. It's too distracting.
EMMA	Why do you always end up targeting kids?
GRAHAM	(*shrug*) You'd be surprised how influential they are.
EMMA	No, I wouldn't.
PAUL	I'll get rid of it.
GRAHAM	Even in what car their Daddy buys. Plus . . .
KATY	You don't have to do that.
GRAHAM	. . . If you get them young . . . a lot of people buy chocolate bars which remind them of childhood. They become nostalgic over time. It's a whole other dimension.
EMMA	So, you don't need Paul.
GRAHAM	(*beat*) Not sure. Does he need the work?
EMMA	Yes, but . . .
KATY	How was Emma?
EMMA	Too proud to admit it.
PAUL	Not great.
GRAHAM	It's still a dingy little house, isn't it?

KATY	They've got real problems.
GRAHAM	Claustrophobic.
EMMA	And what she's done . . . it's terribly . . . sterile, somehow.
PAUL	She said to me 'the human being is not a happy bunny'.
EMMA	They're not happy. That's obvious.
KATY	They need marriage guidance counselling.
GRAHAM	The best way to get what you want is to want what you've got.

(*Phone call.* PAUL *exits to answer it.* KATY *yawns, stretches. We hear, distantly,* PAUL'S *side of the conversation.*)

GRAHAM	Katy looks . . . tired..
EMMA	(*stares*) What d'you mean? Old?
GRAHAM	No. Tired. (*Beat.*) How old is she? Older than you? (*She stares at him, open-mouthed.*) What?
EMMA	Of course she's older than me!
GRAHAM	I mean, much older.
EMMA	Yes, she's much older! She's late forties!
GRAHAM	Really?
EMMA	Mid forties anyway.
GRAHAM	Mid forties. Right.

(*Pause.* EMMA *is still staring.*)

EMMA	I can't believe you said that.

GRAHAM	(*shrug*) Well, she looks young to me.
EMMA	You just said she looks old.
GRAHAM	No, I didn't; I said 'tired'.

> (KATY *is trying to eavesdrop on* PAUL'S *conversation, becoming slightly concerned by his tone.*)

GRAHAM	Do I look old?

(*Pause.*)

EMMA	No.
GRAHAM	I feel old. (*Beat.*) Maybe a bit . . . menopausal. (*Pause.* EMMA *stares, rather thrown.*) I have this . . . sometimes, this overwhelming sense of . . . pointlessness.
EMMA	(*beat*) Pointlessness? (*Pause.*) You think there's no point? (*Beat.*) To what?
GRAHAM	Um . . .

(*Pause.* EMMA *sighs, gets up and walks out.* GRAHAM *and* KATY *are left, both concerned about their partners offstage.*)

GRAHAM	EMMA?

(PAUL *enters, thoughtful.*)

KATY	Who was that?
PAUL	Agent. (*Beat.*) They passed on *Blue Penguin*.
KATY	(*genuinely shocked, hurt*) No.
PAUL	It's okay.

(PAUL *paces slowly.* KATY *watches him.*)

(EMMA, *carrying a few plates and cups, walks through towards the kitchen.*)

EMMA: I'm sorry. I'm just not sure I can cope with anyone else's problems at the moment.

(*She exits to the kitchen.*)

KATY: What's wrong with these people?

PAUL: (*shrug*) I'm not really surprised.

GRAHAM: You told me to talk about my feelings!

PAUL: (*brave face*) It doesn't have to be published. I didn't write it to be published. I mean, that wasn't the main aim. It was a ... personal project, as much as anything ...

(PAUL *wanders upstage and contemplates Mr Happy. Pause.*)

(EMMA *is making quite a bit of noise in the kitchen.*)

KATY: I can't believe it.

PAUL: Doesn't matter.

GRAHAM: What the hell are you doing?

PAUL: Success. Fame and fortune. They're not important.

KATY: I know, but ...

PAUL: (*as if trying to convince himself*) It's people. It's family, friends ... community. And work, the quality of the work, the enjoyment of it, not the result of it. It's not success; it's purpose, and meaning. It's being, not having. That's what Graham doesn't get. That's what the chocolate people don't get. This consumer culture idea that happiness is about cramming as much selfish indulgence into life as possible! It's not! It's much more profound than that.

(*A child is heard crying over the baby monitor.*)

GRAHAM Fuck . . .

(KATY *walks over to* PAUL *and places a hand on his shoulder. Pause.*)

(DAISY *enters with the 'get your baby to sleep' book.*)

PAUL Can you give me a minute?

(KATY *is slightly taken aback. Pause.*)

KATY Yes. Sure.

(*She exits.* PAUL *stands, staring at Mr Happy. He sighs heavily. His mood begins to darken.*)

DAISY Graham?

GRAHAM (*looks up*) Oh, hi.

DAISY I got this book for you. (*She hands it to him.*)

GRAHAM Oh, wow. (*Smile.*) That's fantastic. (EMMA *appears in the doorway.*)

DAISY I heard it was, like . . . recommended.

GRAHAM (*looks at her, rather surprised*) That's really sweet of you.

DAISY It's okay.

(Looks between DAISY, GRAHAM *and* EMMA.*)*

*(*KATY *enters.* PAUL *is unaware of her presence.)*

PAUL *(to Mr Happy)* Who are you grinning at? *(Beat.)* You smug piece of shit.

(He makes to punch Mr Happy in the face.)

KATY Sweetheart?

*(*PAUL *stops. He turns and stares at her.)*

KATY Are you okay?

*(*DAISY *exits, then* EMMA. GRAHAM *begins flicking through the book.)*

(Pause.)

PAUL Why did you carry on eating that biscuit?

(Pause.)

KATY What biscuit?

(Pause.)

PAUL Forget it. Never mind. (KATY *is staring, frowning. Pause.)* Anything on telly tonight?

(Blackout.)

ACT TWO

Scene One

Night. GRAHAM *and* EMMA *are sitting, nervously, listening to the baby monitor. They are both anxious, but* EMMA *more so, apparently.*

> *There is a 'chocolate fountain' on the coffee table along with a plate of strawberries and other fruit and a half-full bottle of champagne in an ice bucket. Also a chocolate bar wrapper lies nearby.*

GRAHAM (*checks watch*) That's . . . thirty minutes.

> (*Eventually,* KATY *leads* PAUL *into the room. He is wearing a blindfold. They are both holding glasses of champagne.*)

GRAHAM (*beginning to smile*) Half-an-hour. Fantastic.

> (KATY *positions* PAUL *in front of the coffee table, then turns the machine on. Molten chocolate begins to cascade over the top of the fountain.*)

PAUL (*re: the noise*) Christ, what's that? Is that an electro cap?

GRAHAM He's asleep.

> (KATY *removes his blindfold.*)
>
> PAUL Wow. (*Grin.*) Look at that.

GRAHAM He's really asleep.

KATY What d'you think?

PAUL It's not Graham's chocolate?

ACT TWO

KATY: No, it's not. Try some.

(GRAHAM *puts his ear against the baby monitor as* PAUL *and* KATY *eat chocolate and strawberries.*)

GRAHAM: Who'd have thought it would be so easy?

PAUL: How indulgent . . .

(PAUL *sits on a chair.* KATY *reclines into the sofa.*)

EMMA: That's amazing.

KATY: See, you like a bit of indulgence occasionally.

GRAHAM: He's fast asleep, he really is.

PAUL: Oh, sure. (*He pours himself some more champagne.*)

(GRAHAM *performs a brief little dance of celebration.* EMMA *manages a smile, though she expects to hear crying at any moment.*)

(KATY, *staring seductively at* PAUL, *undoes a few shirt buttons and begins using a strawberry to drip molten chocolate onto her chest.* PAUL *stares, rather surprised.*)

GRAHAM: Looks like we have some quality time here.

(PAUL *switches off the machine and moves slowly over to* KATY *as* GRAHAM *sits.* PAUL *licks some chocolate from* KATY'S *chest, then kisses her.*)

GRAHAM: How fantastic . . .

	(PAUL *breaks off from foreplay momentarily to check the chocolate wrapper.*)
KATY	What are you doing?
PAUL	Nothing, just . . .
	(*He continues kissing her, but* KATY *is preoccupied.*)
EMMA	(*checks watch*) He's asleep at nine o'clock.
GRAHAM	I know. Extraordinary.
	(*They continue to listen to the baby monitor.*)
	(KATY *breaks off.*)
KATY	What were you looking at?
PAUL	Nothing. The wrapper.
KATY	Why?
PAUL	It's not fair trade. (*Beat.*) But that's fine.
	(KATY *stares. He tries to kiss her but she resists.*)
GRAHAM	So, what d'you think?
KATY	It's not? (*She checks the wrapper.*)
GRAHAM	What shall we do?
PAUL	Well, most aren't. It's not a problem. (*Pause.*) I'm sorry, I didn't mean to . . .
KATY	No, that's okay. Graham's isn't either?

PAUL	No, of course. So, that's a dilemma for me. I checked the costing. It works out that the cocoa producers, in Ghana, they'd get about six per cent of the price of the bar, which is –
KATY	Six?!
PAUL	Yeah, five or six, which is not too bad, so . . .

(GRAHAM *and* EMMA *are sitting in silence.*)

KATY	Six per cent! That's appalling!
PAUL	Really? Well, it's partly because only twenty per cent of the bar is cocoa anyway. Generally, English chocolate is cheap and nasty. Although not as bad as American which tastes like vomit. (KATY *stares.*) See, that's the fallacy of the free market and consumer sovereignty and all that. Doesn't exist. There are big corporate monopolies who spend a tonne of money on advertising. And it works. (KATY *begins wiping the chocolate off her chest.*) You can convince a whole nation that they prefer chocolate which tastes of sick. Why are you doing that?
KATY	Well, I couldn't get a man to lick it off. (*Beat.*) I've been trying all day. Postman, milkman. You were my last hope.
PAUL	I could get into it.
KATY	(*she stares, repressing irritation*) What would that take? (*Beat.*) If you give me a week or two . . . I'll track down some posh fair trade chocolate. Have myself dipped in it.

PAUL	I'm sorry, I didn't mean to ...
KATY	No, it's okay. It's fine.
GRAHAM	Shall I see what's on the box?
EMMA	Um ...
KATY	I'm not sure I'm really ... in the mood anyway.
EMMA	Keep the volume down.

(GRAHAM *turns on the TV with a remote control and begins flicking through the channels.*)

PAUL	I've got to work. We need the money.
KATY	(*re: the chocolate fountain*) This didn't cost anything.
PAUL	No, that's fine.
KATY	About half as much as your coffee maker.
PAUL	I didn't say anything.
KATY	I know what you're thinking.
PAUL	I was thinking about the house.
KATY	What's wrong with it?
PAUL	Nothing. But it's not ours. We don't own it. (*Beat.*) Graham owns it.
KATY	(*frown*) What?
PAUL	He has investments with HSBC worth more than our house.
KATY	(*beat*) How d'you know that?

PAUL	Daisy told me. Since the value of this place dropped, our mortgage is almost ninety per cent. That's nine tenths!
KATY	I know what ninety per cent is.
PAUL	(*over, pacing from one side of the room to the other*) One, two, three, four, five, six, seven, eight, nine! (*He is almost at the other side of the room.*) The last step is ours! We own this much (*Indicates the distance with his hands.*) of our living room! The bank, and Graham, own the rest of it.
KATY	Graham does not own this house. He has no legal rights over it. That's nonsense.
PAUL	I read this article on the internet. Produced by the IMF. It's extraordinary.
KATY	I'm not interested.
	(PAUL *is thrown by her uncharacteristic belligerence.*)
GRAHAM	Not much on . . .
PAUL	Well, very briefly . . .
KATY	Would you rather talk about the IMF than make love to me?
	(*Beat.*)
PAUL	No. Of course not.
	(*Beat.*)
KATY	You're not in the mood.

PAUL	You said that. I didn't say that.
KATY	Because I thought you didn't want to.
PAUL	Why?
KATY	Paul, we just started and you broke off to check the chocolate wrapper.

(*Pause.*)

PAUL	Listen, let's just do it, shall we? (*He quickly removes his trousers.*)
KATY	(*courageous*) Are you still attached to Emma?
PAUL	(*beat*) What?!
KATY	You talk about Graham all the time. It makes me think you still have feelings for Emma.
PAUL	Oh, for Christ's sake . . . (*Beat.*) You know that's not true.
KATY	I don't think we're very good at talking. (*They hold each other's gaze.*) I mean, we don't discuss things, confront things, do we?
PAUL	Like what?
KATY	Like the biscuit.
PAUL	(*pause*) What biscuit? (*Beat.*) I thought you wanted to have sex. (*Pause. She just stares.*) I reckon we're a lot better at talking than most people.

(GRAHAM *and* EMMA *sit, staring at the television. At intervals,* GRAHAM *flicks through some more channels.*)

PAUL   The reason I talk about Graham is that he represents so much..

KATY   (*cuts him off*) Tell me about the biscuit.

PAUL   What biscuit?! You want to talk about biscuits?!

KATY   No, I don't want to talk about –

PAUL   (*over*) You asked me about Emma and Graham. You're changing the subject.

KATY   I'm not asking you to tell me your favourite biscuit. I want to talk about –

PAUL   (*over*) Listen for a minute. Let me tell you what the IMF said.

KATY   I don't give a shit about the IMF.

PAUL   (*louder*) It's relevant to Graham! You asked me why I keep talking about Graham! Let me tell you why! (*Beat.* KATY *stares.*) The IMF have been inflicting unfettered free-market capitalism on the world for fifty years during which time income inequality has gone through the roof. Forget about Ghana for a minute 'cause that's poverty . . . off the scale. Just look at the UK. In 1980, the richest one per cent in this country took six per cent of total income. By 2005 they were taking sixteen per cent! In America, they're over twenty-three per cent. Almost a quarter of all income! But never mind the essential unfairness, the injustice of all that.

	The IMF are now saying that income inequality caused the banking crisis!
KATY	This is not talking.
PAUL	(*over*) If poor people like us still lived in Victorian slums, it wouldn't be a problem. But we don't. We've been borrowing money to pay for homes and lifestyles we can't afford! Not only has income inequality doubled, household debt has also doubled. And Graham is personally responsible. He's been peddling this dream of consumer utopia, of domestic Shangri-La, available to all. Because we all deserve it, don't we? We're entitled to live in a huge house. And to fill it full of consumer crap.
KATY	Like chocolate fountains.
PAUL	Because that's the path to happiness! And if you can't afford it, the bank will lend you the cash. They'll make it as easy as they can. And governments will help them. Because we've all got to keep spending! We have to keep the economy growing! That's why we're here on this planet!
KATY	(*re: the fountain*) Well, I apologise for buying this but I like it.
PAUL	(*over*) More and more stuff is produced and we all have to keep buying it, even those of us who don't have any money!
	(KATY *turns on the chocolate fountain and eats chocolate with her fingers.*)

PAUL	So this is what happens. Graham gives all his advertising cash to the bank and the bank give it to us to buy a house we can't afford! Same thing happened in America. The rich had all these unregulated investments backed by the debts of poor people. It's unsustainable. When the poor can't pay their debts, the bank can't pay the rich people. Everything falls apart! Governments have to bail out the banks with public money, so Graham can get his money back and the bankers can get their bonuses back. Now the whole country is in debt. And people like us pay for it! (*Beat.*) This is not . . . resentment or misanthropy talking! These are real problems! And how I feel about my fucking iPhone has very little to do with anything at all!
	(*He takes his iPhone out of his pocket and moves to throw it against the wall.*)
KATY	Paul!
	(*He stops himself. Beat. He drops the iPhone into his champagne glass.* KATY *stares at it, shocked, open-mouthed. Pause. She switches off the chocolate fountain.*)
KATY	For Christ's sake . . .
PAUL	I can't afford it anyway. The monthly payments are too high.
	(*She stares at him.*)
GRAHAM	How come, the more channels you get, the less there is to watch?

KATY	What is the matter with you?
PAUL	We are not middle-class. We cannot afford iPhones. And we can't afford this house. I'm a failed writer; you're a nursery school teacher. We are poor. (*He puts his trousers back on.*) And I don't blame you; I blame myself. I think . . . To some extent, I sold myself to you as some kind of success story.
KATY	(*beat*) Paul, I'm not stupid. I never saw you as a success story.
PAUL	(*looks at her, slightly deflated*) Didn't you?
KATY	Tell me about the biscuit. (PAUL *sighs. Pause.*) Talk to me.
PAUL	It's nothing. I wish I'd never mentioned it.
KATY	It's clearly something.
	(*Pause.*)
PAUL	I think . . . sometimes, for no good reason, I worry about . . . what my . . . life amounts to. And if I'll really be missed and all that, you know? It's an existential . . .
KATY	What's that got to do with the biscuit?
PAUL	(*beat*) Not much. I suppose, in the moment, when you took another bite of your biscuit . . . it just . . .
KATY	(*frown*) When I what?

PAUL	(*beat*) When I told you about the misdiagnosis. (*Beat.*) You took another bite.
KATY	No, I didn't!
PAUL	(*beat*) You did actually.
KATY	I was eating the biscuit when you told me!
PAUL	Yeah, and then you took another bite.
KATY	No, I didn't. I most certainly did not.
PAUL	(*sigh*) Oh, okay. It looked, to me, like you did and, for a moment, it just struck me as some kind of . . . displacement activity . . . I wish I hadn't mentioned..
KATY	Displacement activity?
PAUL	Like scratching your head when you can't decide.
KATY	Can't decide what?

(EMMA, *with one ear directed at the baby monitor, exits to the kitchen.*)

PAUL	(*beat*) I think it's derived from animal behaviour studies. You know, when a bird or whatever doesn't know how to react to a situation, it might peck at something or groom itself.
KATY	(*inwardly fuming*) If you're trying to suggest that I was disappointed that I wouldn't be getting the life insurance . . .
PAUL	(*getting frustrated*) No, not that. Listen, I've thought it through. It's

	not a big deal. I think when you come to terms with being on your own again and then, suddenly, you're not going to be on your own, I don't think that's really, you know, I think it's unrealistic to imagine that would be one hundred per cent good news!
KATY	(*beat*) The fact that you're not going to die of cancer . . .
PAUL	(*sigh*) Let's not . . .
KATY	Is not one hundred per cent good news.
PAUL	It's nothing . . . I wish I hadn't . . .
KATY	Sometimes I really wonder about you.
PAUL	You know, the fact that you're making such a big deal . . . Wonder what exactly?
KATY	That confirms your suspicion, I suppose.
PAUL	Please can we forget it?
KATY	The fact that I'm absolutely livid – about the appalling accusation that I was looking forward to your premature death –
PAUL	I never said that.
KATY	– makes you think it must be true! Is that what you're saying?!
PAUL	(*pause, stares*) I'm not saying anything.
	(*Beat.* KATY *exits.* PAUL *contemplates his iPhone in the champagne glass.*)

(*We hear a door slam, but* PAUL *does not react to it,* GRAHAM *does.*)

GRAHAM What are you doing?!

EMMA (*off*) Sorry.

GRAHAM For Christ's sake!

(KATY *enters, wearing an overcoat.*)

PAUL Where are you going?

KATY By the way, I just think – if it was Emma smearing chocolate on her tits – you wouldn't have got up to check the fucking wrapper!

(*She exits. A moment later, another door slam.* GRAHAM *doesn't react.*)

(EMMA *enters.* GRAHAM *is staring at her. Pause. She sits.*)

(PAUL *takes his iPhone out of the glass.*)

GRAHAM (*re: the door slam*) Why did you do that?

EMMA (*beat*) Do what? (*Pause.*) It was an accident.

(*Pause.*)

(PAUL'S *iPhone is dead. He drops it onto the fruit plate then takes the plate and the chocolate fountain out to the kitchen.*)

GRAHAM (*irritated*) Are we . . . Listen. What are we doing? D'you want to watch something or . . . shall we have a . . . conversation?

EMMA Conversation?

GRAHAM   Yes, a conversation.

           (*Pause.*)

                              (PAUL *returns, picks up the ice
                              bucket and glasses and returns to the
                              kitchen.*)

EMMA   You start.

           (*Pause.* GRAHAM *continues staring, scrutinising,
           making* EMMA *uncomfortable. Then we hear baby
           crying. Pause.*)

EMMA   Stop staring.

           (*Pause.* EMMA *leaves the room.*)

                              Scene Two

Morning. KATY *is pacing in an agitated state. She has been
crying.*

                              PAUL *is sitting, scrawling some
                              words onto the pages of a notebook.*

It seems as if they might be in the same room, until GRAHAM
enters with a glass of water.

GRAHAM   Here you go. (*Hands her the glass.*)

                              (*Doorbell.* PAUL *lifts himself slowly,
                              then exits.*)

KATY   It was just . . . Such a shock. I didn't know how to
           react. And I thought, well, I've got to be happy
           about this. That's the obvious . . . And I just took
           another bite of the biscuit.

GRAHAM   What biscuit?

KATY Christ, this is turning into a migraine. D'you have any pain-killers?

GRAHAM Oh, sure, we have . . . various. Which do you prefer?

(GRAHAM *exits to the kitchen,* KATY *follows.*)

(DAISY *enters, followed by* PAUL.)

DAISY (*resolute*) I'm going home. I'm going to tell Mum I'm not doing the placement. Or the business degree.

PAUL Where have you been?

DAISY Wayne's. I've decided; I want to do politics.

PAUL Politics?!

DAISY What's wrong with that?

PAUL (*beat*) I don't know. Is that really . . . vocational?

DAISY Christ, you sound like Mum!

PAUL You've never been bothered about politics.

DAISY (*fast, vigorous*) No, exactly! That's the whole point! There's this awesome website, you should check it out, it's all about politics, about how there's no real difference anymore, all the parties are selling the same shit, you know, like 'we'll look after the economy better than they will', so there's no, like, ideology anymore, no big ideas, it's all spin, you know, like advertising, how to make your product look different from everyone else's, so you get

	politicians who don't really believe in anything, they're just in it for the career, or the fucking expenses! In the old days, you'd support one party and, like, hate the others, but now you just hate all of them, especially if you're my age. Young people used to think 'maybe I can change the world', now they don't give a shit, you know?, they just want to be famous or something.
PAUL	I agree with you.
DAISY	Then what the fuck are you talking about?
PAUL	(*becoming annoyed*) All right, calm down.
DAISY	It's all about to change, I mean, it's changing already because it's so obvious, this boom and bust capitalism doesn't work and Globalisation doesn't work. I'll lend you Wayne's book. The rich are getting richer and the poor are getting poorer, the climate's getting worse and worse, it's, like, so obvious now, you can't let big business run the world, people have to take power back, which will mean, like, real politics, you know, real democracy.
PAUL	Did you say Wayne's book?
DAISY	Yeah, he's got a few you could read.
PAUL	He's reading? (DAISY's *mouth falls open*.) I mean, he's –
DAISY	Of course he's reading!

PAUL	I didn't mean that! I mean, he's reading, like, serious books.
DAISY	(*angry*) As opposed to what, the Beano?! He's an activist! In the anti-globalisation movement! He's not stupid!
PAUL	Is that why he's got a criminal record?
DAISY	(*beat, stares*) Does she tell you everything?! (*Beat.*) He broke a window on a demo! That's all. There were all these news people, these photographers egging him on. They love a broken window. They don't give a shit about the issues but they love a broken window.

(*Her mobile phone rings.*)

PAUL	Listen, don't tell your mother I told you . . .

(KATY *enters, putting on her coat, about to leave. She is still in an agitated, confused state of mind.*)

DAISY	At least he's doing something, isn't he? Which is more than most people. Even you! What do you actually do? Apart from, like, moan about everything?
PAUL	All right, that's enough!

(DAISY *exits to answer the phone.*)

(GRAHAM *enters.*)

KATY	The problem is . . . When I think back. It was so . . . stale. You know?
GRAHAM	The biscuit?

KATY   What?

GRAHAM   The biscuit was stale?

KATY   No, Paul and I. The relationship.

GRAHAM   What about the biscuit?

KATY   (*stares at him*) Why is the biscuit so fucking important?

GRAHAM   I've no idea! You said you argued over a biscuit.

KATY   Did I? Christ. (*She sits and tries to control her breathing.*) I'm sorry. I'm so sorry.

GRAHAM   It's okay.

KATY   I'm over-breathing. I used to have panic attacks in the bad old days.

GRAHAM   Are you okay?

KATY   When we got the diagnosis . . . The cancer. It was terrible. But there's no doubt – it brought us closer. And I felt needed. I had some . . . purpose. And everyone at work was so nice. (*Pause.*) And then, he was okay again and – I didn't want him to die, obviously – but I didn't want things to go back to how they were. Do you have a paper bag?

GRAHAM   (*pause*) A what?

KATY   A paper bag.

GRAHAM   I don't think so. Carrier bag? (*He exits to the kitchen.*)

KATY   Not plastic.

GRAHAM   (*off*) We don't do plastic bags.

KATY He thinks it was because of the money; it was nothing to do with the money.

(*Enters with a reusable textile carrier bag with supermarket logo emblazoned on it.*)

KATY You know, I read his book, his 'happiness' book, before I met him. (*Beat.*) He wasn't really what I was expecting.

GRAHAM Right.

KATY I think, to some extent, I fell in love with Mr Happy, you know? The cardboard cut-out; not the real man.

(*She puts the bag over her head and concentrates on her breathing.*)

GRAHAM Yes, I can see how that would be . . . disappointing.

(*Their hands touch.*)

KATY Apparently you shouldn't do this. But it always works for me.

(KATY *takes* GRAHAM'S *hand and holds onto it.*)

(DAISY *bursts in.*)

DAISY (*delighted*) Dad, your plan worked!

PAUL Sorry?

DAISY That was Mum. She's staying with Granny tonight 'cause she fell out with Graham! Sounds like it's serious. So, it worked! Your plan worked!

PAUL What plan?

DAISY Give them the baby book to break them up quicker!

KATY	I should go home.
PAUL	Oh, no, that's not, that wasn't my intention . . .
DAISY	Total genius! She wouldn't be staying with Gran unless there was real trouble! That's so awesome! And they can't gang up on me and make me do business studies!
PAUL	Nobody's ganging up.
DAISY	I better go. Where's Katy anyhow?
PAUL	Not here. (*Beat.*) At the moment.

(GRAHAM *and* KATY *are still holding hands.*)

(PAUL *sits next to* GRAHAM *and* KATY *on the sofa.*)

KATY	Where's Emma?
DAISY	Where is she?
GRAHAM	I'm not sure.
PAUL	We had a . . . row.
GRAHAM	We had a . . . scene . . . last night.
DAISY	(*stares*) For real?
KATY	Why? (*She removes the carrier bag.*)
PAUL	She stayed with her sister last night.
GRAHAM	Lots of reasons.
DAISY	(*mouth falls open*) Really?! (*Slight smile.*)

GRAHAM	(*sigh*) Too many to . . .
PAUL	Don't look so pleased.
DAISY	No, I'm not pleased. it's just . . . totally weird. The coincidence. Don't you think?
GRAHAM	She seems obsessed with this . . . female colleague of mine . . .
DAISY	I can't imagine her rowing.
PAUL	Oh, yeah, she really lost it.
GRAHAM	For some reason. I mean, infidelity is not my thing . . . (*He and* KATY *hold each other's gaze.*)
PAUL	I think, sometimes, I provoke her.
DAISY	Why?
PAUL	Get a reaction. I don't know. It's not nice.
DAISY	Sorry. Are you upset?
(GRAHAM *and* KATY *kiss.*)	
PAUL	(*beat*) No, I'm fine. (*Beat.*) We'll be fine. I'm sure we will. I mean, most relationships have these . . . ups and downs . . . Like your mother and Graham. It's normal. (*He rises from the sofa as* KATY *and* GRAHAM *recline into where he was sitting.*)
PAUL	And the baby book . . . It really wasn't my intention . . .
DAISY	Don't be so modest.

                    (*Pause.* PAUL *remembers something.*)

PAUL   Oh! Those balloons arrived.

DAISY   Oh, brilliant!

PAUL   Yeah, they look really good actually.

                    (PAUL *exits; she follows.*)

DAISY   Cool.

(KATY *and* GRAHAM *begin to make love on the sofa as the lights fade.*)

Scene Three

Evening. Stage empty. EMMA'S *mobile phone, on the coffee table, begins to play 'Be My Baby'. After a few moments,* EMMA *enters in an expensive-looking dress, carrying one or two accessories. She is stressed, running late.*

EMMA   (*under her breath*) Fucking hell . . . (*Answers the phone.*) Hello? (*Pause.*) I don't know why you keep calling me. How did you get this number? (*Pause.*) Well, I don't know who told you that but it's wrong so please take this number off your database. (DAISY *enters, with overnight case which she places near the door.*) And my address too. Please stop sending me things because they go straight in the recycling. (*Beat.*) Thank you.

        (*She hangs up and stands, thinking, frowning.*)

DAISY   You look cool.

EMMA   (*preoccupied*) Thanks. (*Beat.*) Tell me about your party.

DAISY   Why? You were there.

EMMA   I left at eight.

DAISY   After making a huge fuss.

EMMA   I didn't make a fuss.

DAISY   You were bursting balloons.

EMMA   I only burst a few. I just couldn't believe he'd do that! On your eighteenth birthday! Balloons with depressing messages!

DAISY   Like I said, Mum, you just don't get it.

EMMA   I do get it. And it's so typical of him. Maybe I know him better than you do. (*Beat.*) Can I get rid of them now? They're cluttering up the kitchen.

DAISY   (*shrug*) Whatever. Where are you going?

EMMA   Dinner with the Delamere's. (*She exits to the kitchen.*)

DAISY   Oh, God.

EMMA   (*off*) I couldn't get out of it. (*Beat.*) I mean, we couldn't get out of it.

DAISY   I'm just off.

EMMA   (*off*) Okay. Have a nice time. (EMMA *enters with some estate agent's details for a few houses.*) Why would Graham give my contact details to an estate agent?

DAISY   He didn't. I did.

(*Pause.* EMMA *stares, taken aback.*)

DAISY   (*matter-of-fact*) You said you wanted to move. (*Beat.*) A few months ago. After one of your big rows.

EMMA   I wasn't serious.

DAISY   (*shrug*) Well, you said it.

(EMMA *glances at the house details.*)

DAISY That one's awesome. You could easily afford that.

EMMA (*beat*) With what? (*Beat.*) You mean, if I got divorced . . .

DAISY I know how loaded he is. It's a small fortune, isn't it? You'd have to get a good lawyer. Have a look at the cottage; there's a really cool office in the garden; Dad would love it. Anyway, I got to go.

(EMMA *stands in her way.*)

EMMA Daisy, what are you thinking of?

(DAISY *stares.* EMMA'S *amazement begins to turn into anger.*)

EMMA Who is this for, this house? What are you imagining?

DAISY They're just suggestions.

EMMA I thought you wanted your own place.

DAISY (*shrug*) I don't know. But I don't want to live with Graham.

EMMA Do you imagine the world revolves around you?! That you can have whatever you like?!

DAISY What's your problem?

EMMA You never gave Graham a chance!

DAISY Oh, it's my fault, now?!

EMMA (*holds up the house details*) This is not just about you! This involves other people!

DAISY Get out of my way! (*She pushes* EMMA.)

EMMA Don't you dare!

DAISY (*loud, emotional*) I'm just trying to put right what I messed up! Don't you get it?!

(*Pause.* EMMA *stares, thrown by this statement.* DAISY *wants to leave before she cries.*)

EMMA What d'you mean?

DAISY Just get out of my way! I'm going! And I'm never coming back!

(DAISY *storms out. We hear the front door slam.* EMMA *stands, shocked. She notices* DAISY'S *case. She sits, waiting for* DAISY *to return, thinking hard. Finally, we hear the front door open, then* DAISY *enters.*)

DAISY Forgot my case.

EMMA What did you mean by that?

(DAISY *picks up her case and thinks about leaving, but doesn't. Pause.*)

EMMA You didn't mess anything up.

DAISY I was a spoilt brat. I know I was. You don't have to tell me.

EMMA You weren't that bad. And, anyway, I blame myself.

DAISY Oh, bullshit.

EMMA Daisy, your father and I . . . The fact that we split up had nothing to do with you.

DAISY (*hovering in the doorway, case in hand*) Yeah, right.

EMMA You don't believe me?

DAISY	You shouldn't have had another child! You should have learned your lesson.
EMMA	(*frown*) What d'you mean? (*Beat.*) Jack's fine. He's not a problem.
DAISY	(*looks at* EMMA *like she's gone mad*) Are you serious?
EMMA	Granny says he's good as gold. Whenever he stays with her, he sleeps right through.
DAISY	She's up to her old tricks. Trying to make you feel like a bad mother.
EMMA	(*sigh*) No, she's not doing that. I don't think so.
DAISY	You kept telling me Jack was the problem.
EMMA	Well, if I say things . . . in the heat of the moment . . . About Jack. Or about Granny.
DAISY	On like a daily basis.
EMMA	Or about moving house. Daisy, darling, I'm serious. Jack's not the problem. I think it was . . . a distraction somehow . . . from the real . . .
DAISY	Unconscious avoidance strategy.
	(EMMA *looks at her. Then realisation.*)
EMMA	Oh, God, did your father tell you that?
DAISY	(*beat, shrug*) Don't know.
EMMA	Have you been talking to him?
DAISY	(*beat, like her mother's stupid*) Yes. Guilty.
EMMA	About buying a house?
DAISY	No. He had nothing to do with that. I got to go.

EMMA   Did you change my ring tone?

DAISY   (*beat*) I thought you'd like it.

EMMA   (*sigh*) Sweetheart, listen to me, it wasn't your fault.

DAISY   If you say so.

EMMA   Your father had an affair.

DAISY   (*beat*) He what?

EMMA   That's the reason. At least, that's the main . . . (*Sigh.*) Well, I don't know anymore, what happened, but whatever happened, it was us; it was nothing to do with you.

DAISY   (*over*) I don't want to know about your . . . private life, that's totally gross.

(*She leaves swiftly.* EMMA *sighs heavily and sits, thinking hard.* GRAHAM *enters wearing suit, tie undone, and EEG cap. He is carrying the laptop.*)

GRAHAM   You arguing again?

(EMMA *contemplates him with some contempt. He sits. He seems depressed.*)

EMMA   If you want to know whether chocolate gives you more of a 'brain buzz' than dinner with the Delamere's . . . I could tell you that myself. It's a no-brainer. (*He stares.*) I'm not going if you're wearing that.

(*He studies the laptop.*)

GRAHAM   Maybe I can't . . . express my feelings very well. But I can show you my brain.

(EMMA *glances at the brain image on the laptop which shows more red areas than blue.*)

EMMA   What does all that red mean?

GRAHAM Brain activity.

EMMA   Right. So, you're alive.

GRAHAM Looks like it's about to explode. (*Pause.*) We did this brain-storming session . . . Everyone had to think about what made them happy, apart from chocolate. Eventually, we had this long list . . . Walking in the woods, babies laughing, meeting friends in the pub, singing in church, playing tennis, blah, blah . . .

(*Pause.* EMMA *stares.*)

EMMA   What did you say?

GRAHAM I couldn't think of anything. (*Beat.*) Apart from sex. (*Beat.*) And a good game of Scrabble.

EMMA   (*beat*) Simultaneous?

(*He ignores her and continues to stare at the image of his brain.*)

GRAHAM So, all that activity . . . I'm not sure what it's all for. (*Beat.*) I've worked so hard all my life. But . . . if that's all there is . . .

(*He stares at her, then he begins to cry.* EMMA *watches.*)

EMMA   Don't cry with that thing on. You'll short circuit. Your head'll explode.

(*He composes himself quickly and removes the cap.*)

GRAHAM You don't want to know, do you?

EMMA   (*sigh*) Maybe it's a bit late . . .

GRAHAM You're too wrapped up in your own problems.

(She stares. He stares back.)

EMMA Graham, they're not my problems! They're Jack's or Daisy's or Mums...

GRAHAM I'm your husband. Where am I on the list?

(Pause.)

EMMA *(shrug)* Maybe I thought you'd look after me. *(Pause.)* I'm too tired to argue. *(She checks her watch.)* The Delamere's are waiting.

GRAHAM Are you ready?

EMMA As I'll ever be.

(GRAHAM ties his tie. EMMA puts her high-heeled shoes on.)

GRAHAM Oh, your idiot ex-husband wrote this ridiculous copy about Hitler and Eva Braun eating chocolate in the bunker in Berlin. *(EMMA smiles slightly.)* And he sent it direct to the client. Then someone sent it on and it started spreading, like a fucking email virus. Everyone thought it was a serious proposal from this loony advertising agency. So, we had to hang him out to dry. We said it was all his work, acting alone. *(Beat.)* He might never work in advertising again. Do you need make-up?

(EMMA stares at him.)

EMMA I'm wearing make-up!

GRAHAM You don't look well.

EMMA *(beat)* I've hardly slept. What d'you expect?

GRAHAM You should see a doctor. You've aged about five years in twelve months.

(GRAHAM *moves to the door.* EMMA *is frozen, fuming. He turns and stares. Doorbell.*)

GRAHAM Who the hell's that?

(EMMA *exits to the kitchen, purposefully. He sighs.*)

GRAHAM What are you doing?

EMMA (*off*) Clearly I need some of your expensive face cream!

(*She enters with the tub of face cream and begins smearing it on her face in huge dollops.*)

EMMA There! How's that?! Is that better?! (*She covers her face in the cream.*) Do I look younger yet?!

(*They stare, immobile for a moment. Pause. Another doorbell.*)

GRAHAM I'll tell them you're having a breakdown.

(*He leaves. Pause.* EMMA *discards the tub of cream, sits on the sofa and stares into space.* PAUL *enters tentatively. He looks slightly smarter than usual. He stands and contemplates her with cream all over her face. Pause.*)

PAUL You've got a bit of . . . cream on your face.

EMMA Have I?

(*Pause.*)

PAUL Is this a bad time?

EMMA Not at all.

(EMMA *exits to the kitchen. Pause.* PAUL *looks around at everything, including the cap.*)

PAUL Your husband seemed delighted to see me.

(*No response.* PAUL *picks up the estate agent details.* EMMA *enters, attending to her face with a tea towel. She watches him studying the paperwork.*)

EMMA   Daisy's trying to get me to move out. (PAUL *looks up.*) She gave all my contact details to an estate agent.

PAUL   (*smile*) Really?

EMMA   It's not funny.

PAUL   (*beat*) Why would she do that?

EMMA   (*beat*) You tell me.

PAUL   (*beat*) How would I know?

(*Pause. They stare.*)

PAUL   This one looks great. Huge garden.

EMMA   But not much house.

PAUL   No, well, that's fine. Perfect for downshifting.

EMMA   What's downshifting?

PAUL   Scaling back. You know? Living on less money, using less energy. The garden's ideal for vegetables.

EMMA   (*under-whelmed*) How thrilling.

PAUL   What's that? Is that an outside office?

EMMA   You've just missed her. Daisy, I mean. If that's who...

PAUL   Right.

EMMA	She's sleeping over with a friend. (*Beat.*) Or with Wayne. God help us. She never tells me anymore. By the way, I've got something for you.

(*She exits to the kitchen and returns swiftly with two bin bags filled with about thirty inflated balloons. Each balloon has a statement printed on it: 'Failure is more common than success', 'Many will dislike you, whatever you do' and 'The world does not oblige'. She empties the bags at* PAUL's *feet.*)

EMMA	What, in God's name, were you thinking?! (*She picks up a balloon.*) 'Failure is more common than success.'
PAUL	There's a psychologist called Albert Ellis.
EMMA	(*picks up another balloon*) 'Many will dislike you, whatever you do.'
PAUL	He thought people tortured themselves with unrealistic expectations.
EMMA	(*over*) I know; Daisy told me. But, Paul, it's a birthday party! For eighteen year olds! You want to disillusion them all?!
PAUL	They need it more than anyone.
EMMA	I know why you did it. Because it's Graham's do. You wanted to piss all over it. Didn't you?
PAUL	Oh, come on. It was Daisy's do. And it was her idea as much as mine.
EMMA	You're something else.
PAUL	At the time, it seemed entirely appropriate. She was planning a psychology degree . . .
EMMA	Just take your balloons and go.

(Pause. He stares at her. She stares back. He sighs and begins collecting up the balloons.)

EMMA   Apparently, she blames herself. For our divorce.

PAUL   (*shrug*) It's not uncommon.

EMMA   Did you know?!

PAUL   (*beat*) No. I suspected.

EMMA   Well, why didn't you talk to her?

PAUL   I have talked to her. Many times.

EMMA   She doesn't know about your affair.

PAUL   (*beat*) Does she know about yours?

EMMA   Yours came first.

PAUL   I don't think it's really that simple.

EMMA   I'm not saying it's simple; I'm saying she should know. (*Pause.*) She knows now anyway.

(Pause.)

PAUL   It's not . . . When you move out. It's not easy to turn your daughter against you. Plus, she's my only fan.

EMMA   Your fan?

PAUL   I'm joking.

EMMA   She's not your fan; she's your daughter.

PAUL   Right. And I was unfaithful to her mother. So she's supposed to hate me.

EMMA   No. But she's not supposed to idolise you.

PAUL   She doesn't idolise me. (*Pause.*) Anyway, she won't now, will she?

(*Pause. PAUL continues collecting balloons. EMMA sits and discards her shoes disdainfully. PAUL studies one of the balloons.*)

PAUL   My novel was rejected.

EMMA   (*pause*) Send it somewhere else.

PAUL   I'm running out of publishers. (*Pause. He sits and reads from the balloon.*) 'The world does not oblige'. (*Pause.*) I invested too much, you know. In writing. (*Pause. EMMA is listening.*) At a certain point, I started to believe I couldn't be happy unless I was a successful novelist. (*Beat.*) I don't know how that happened. I'm really annoyed with myself. It goes against everything I believe in. (*Beat.*) I got sucked in by the ... success thing ...

EMMA   Most people do. (*Pause.*) For what it's worth ... Graham says, "the best way to get what you want is to want what you've got".

(PAUL *stares.*)

PAUL   Graham says that?

(*He exits. Pause.*)

EMMA   (*frowning*) Paul?

(*He returns with a copy of his book, 'How to be Happy'. He is looking for a particular page.*)

EMMA   Where did you get that?

PAUL   (*stares*) It's on your bookcase! You didn't know?

EMMA   I forgot. How did you know?

PAUL   Because I noticed it! (*He stares, then continues looking for the page.*) I always notice it. Here!

"The best way to get what you want is to want what you've got."

EMMA Oh, it's in there?

PAUL It's a chapter title!

EMMA Right.

PAUL Don't you know who I am? I'm Mr Fucking Happy!

EMMA No, you're not. You're a novelist.

(*Pause.* PAUL *sits.*)

EMMA I read *Blue Penguin*. Daisy gave it to me.

PAUL Really?

EMMA (*matter-of-fact*) Yeah, I thought it was amazing. I loved it.

PAUL Oh, really? Thank you. I'm not sure it's amazing, but . . . Thanks.

EMMA You never did value my opinion.

(*They stare.*)

PAUL That's not true.

EMMA Isn't it?

PAUL (*pause*) I'm very pleased you read it. I actually . . . I never thought you would. So, that's . . . (*Beat.*) I really appreciate that.

EMMA Well, I loved it. It made me cry. (*Pause.*) You'll have to send it somewhere else. (*Beat.*) Seriously. You have to.

PAUL You know, public recognition . . . and all that . . . I'm glad to say it's not as important – not quite as important – as it used to be.

EMMA	Never the less . . .
	(*They hold each other's gaze until* EMMA *looks away.* PAUL *continues collecting up the balloons.*)
EMMA	Do you really want those?
PAUL	(*beat*) Not really.
EMMA	Well, leave them. (*On her way to the kitchen:*) But you can take these. (*She exits.* PAUL *sits.* EMMA *returns with three large helium balloons with the same three messages, boldly emblazoned. She hands the strings to* PAUL, *then sits opposite him. Pause.*)
PAUL	Where were you going anyway? You're all dressed up.
EMMA	Dinner with the Delamere's. But we had a row. Graham went without me.
PAUL	Oh, right. (*Pause. Courageous:*) D'you want to . . . go for a curry or something?
EMMA	No, I'm fine. (*Beat.*) I could do with some time to myself. The house is empty, for once.
PAUL	Right. (*Beat.*) Okay.

(*Pause. He moves slowly towards the door. Glances between them. Finally, he leaves with the three balloons.* EMMA *listens to the front door close then sits, for a few moments, in quiet contemplation. She picks up a remote control and presses a few buttons. We hear the beginning of 'Be My Baby' by the Ronettes. She listens to the song for a few moments, smiles almost imperceptibly then exits to the kitchen. Soon she returns with another bar of* GRAHAM'S *chocolate, a bottle of rosé wine and a large glass. Approaching the sofa, she is captivated by the song, closes her eyes and moves to the music for a few moments, still clutching the aforementioned objects. Then she sits on the sofa and presses another button on the remote control which turns the music's volume up and up. She pours a glass of wine and begins stuffing her mouth with chocolate. She pulls her knees up to her chest and sits, listening to the music, eyes closed, in a kind of foetal position. We hear the whole song. The lights begin to fade as the music fades.)*